FRIDAY
WAS THE
BOMB

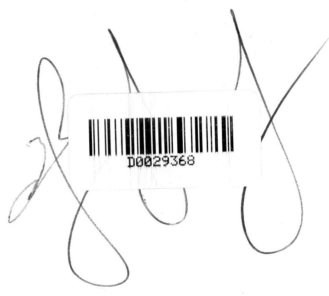

FRIDAY
WAS THE
BOMB

FIVE YEARS IN THE MIDDLE EAST

NATHAN DEUEL

DZANC
BOOKS

DISQUIET

DIS|QUIET

5220 Dexter Ann Arbor Rd.
Ann Arbor, MI 48103
www.dzancbooks.org
www.disquietinternational.org

These essays first appeared, in slightly different form, in the following publications: *Aeon Magazine, Al Jazeera America, The Awl, GQ, Los Angeles Review of Books, The Morning News, The National (U.A.E.), The New Republic, Salon, Slate, St. Petersburg Review,* and *Virginia Quarterly Review.*

Book design: Steven Seighman

ISBN: 978-1-938604-90-4
First edition: April 2014

The publication of this book is made possible with support from the National Endowment for the Arts, and the Michigan Council for Arts and Cultural Affairs.

Printed in the United States of America

10   9   8   7   6   5   4   3   2   1

CONTENTS

4.

5.

For Kelly, who came home

In the dark times, will there also be singing?
Yes, there will be singing.
About the dark times.

—BERTOLT BRECHT

TIMELINE

September 2008   Nathan and Kelly move to Saudi Arabia

June 2009   Daughter Loretta is born at Kingdom Hospital in Riyadh

April 2010   Nathan's dad passes away at Florida's Mayo Clinic

June 2010   Kelly becomes NPR's Baghdad Bureau Chief

March 2011   Unrest spreads to Bahrain, Yemen, Iraq, and Syria

November 2011   Nathan and Loretta move to Beirut

December 2011   Kelly leaves Iraq with the last convoy of U.S. troops; she later joins her family in Beirut

February 2012   Journalists Anthony Shadid and Marie Colvin die in Syria

April 2012   Seven-hour shoot-out on Al Kalaa Street in Beirut

October 2012   Car bombing in Beirut kills head of Lebanese intelligence

June 2013   Nathan and Loretta leave Beirut

August 2013   Kelly files her final report from the Middle East

September 2013   The family moves together to Los Angeles

1

HOLIDAY IN BAGHDAD

The plane smelled of sweat and perfume. Rising to stretch my legs, I surveyed my fellow passengers. Almost all were Iraqis, and there was a preponderance of plastic and/or leopard-print overnight bags. The men had big mustaches and weary eyes. Many of the women wore colored headscarves and seemed to be in their thirties, some of them no doubt returning to Iraq for the first time in years. My wife had just been named NPR's new Baghdad bureau chief. This was my first visit to Iraq, and my first time leaving Istanbul, where I lived with our daughter.

I felt weak in the knees. My mom had flown to Turkey for a visit. She was babysitting so I could take this trip. An Iraqi girl sized me up. "What did you expect?" her eyes seemed to inquire. "Your people fucked us up good." I let my head fall.

Dawn broke as we hit the tarmac. Behind a battered desk stood an Iraqi official armed with a gleaming .45-caliber pistol. I was supposed to meet a guy named Muthana. Without him I'd never get through—anyone who came to Iraq these days needed some kind of sponsor. But in the scrum of men with moustaches, how would I know it was him? My wife, Kelly, had sent me a photo, which I pulled up on my phone. Muthana was a broad-shouldered man, with twin girls sitting on either of his denim-clad knees. In the early morning heat and dust, among the guns and the uniforms, I stared at the picture, realizing that he had left his children early this morning to help *me*.

Muthana recognized me before I recognized him, and he beamed at me like a proud father. He grabbed me by the shoulder with a big hand and pushed me toward an office.

"Wait," he said, and disappeared inside, shutting the door behind him. When he emerged a few minutes later, he had sweat on his brow and a tight smile.

"You have badge?" he said.

"A what?" I said, mystified. "Do I need a badge?" Kelly hadn't said anything about a badge. My stomach fluttered.

Shaking, I took out my wallet and browsed stupidly. I found a gift card from Dunkin' Donuts, a wad of Turkish lira, a canceled credit card, and my Florida driver's license.

Pawing uselessly at the stack of plastic, Muthana wilted. A portly official in a green army uniform stepped forward. He grabbed my wrist and looked into my eyes.

"No badge?" he said, motioning at my wallet. "Look again."

I pawed again through credit cards and old receipts. The official leaned into me with some feeling, looking inside my wallet, his eyebrows raised and his body touching mine. I could feel his warm breath.

"You have nothing?"

I felt the desert heat mounting. What did I have? In the room behind me were several dozen security contractors. For most Americans, moving through the world was to feel a certain invincibility.

But here in Iraq, there was a new feeling: a sense that anything could happen, that we probably deserved whatever came our way. The smoke from a dozen cigarettes swirled, and with a lack of sleep taking effect, I tried not to panic.

"Here," I said, ecstatic, holding my passport open to an old visa. "Saudi Arabia. Journalist. In Arabic. No problem!"

The official patted my wrist, opened his mustached lips in a split of teeth, and with another tenuous agreement between visitor and visited, I was in.

In the beginning, Iraq had seemed like the center of the universe. On a bitterly cold New York day in 2003, I had marched with several hundred thousand others, as much out of a conviction that the war was wrong as that it was inevitable. If we as a nation were going into battle, it felt appropriate for all of us to stand in the cold and suffer. Things got heavy fast. In the first weeks of battle, an old boss of mine lost his life when a Humvee flipped. It was hard to figure out my place in the strange brew of writers, soldiers, pundits, foreigners, and observers. Then people started dying—in numbers far in excess of anything anyone expected. What was the point of all that carnage? What was the role of the journalist? A friend signed up for the infantry and flew to Iraq shortly thereafter. Working at a newspaper in New York, I found myself editing a Very Important Piece about the 1,000th death of a U.S. soldier, then another Very Important Piece about the 2,000th. I wanted to go to Iraq. No matter how skeptical anyone was of the war planning, it's not like anyone *wanted* it all to go badly—and then things got much worse. In the bloodiest years of 2006 and 2007, during the uprisings in towns like Fallujah, we had good friends who went in and out as correspondents, and a few more who served as soldiers. Despite the various personal connections—or perhaps because of them—the war felt further and further away.

I admit that at the height of the chaos, I stopped reading. So many dead dumped in ditches, countless American fuckups, too many tragedies to fathom. *New York Times* ace Dexter Filkins filed another epic frontline report, and I'd drift to the Book Review or the Style Section. In the ensuing years, with the endless grinding of Iraqi parliamentary democracy, various failed coalitions, muddy alliances, car bombs, power outages—it all became just another story.

Then my wife Kelly accepted the job in Baghdad, and Iraq—like it or not—came roaring back into my life.

Seven years and hundreds of thousands of dead later, I stood on the other side of passport control. I was in Iraq. And I was terrified. Kelly held me.

"Don't worry," she said. "You're with me now."

In the baking sun of Baghdad, Kelly and I walked across a surprisingly normal airport parking lot—no craters, no blood, no bullet casings—to an armored truck that appeared to have half-inch glass windows. The front door felt like it was made of solid iron. The driver, Ahmed, gave me a big smile and roared the engine through the first of what would come to seem like an endless series of checkpoints.

"Very thick glass," he said. "We have one hour—even if they hold the gun very close."

I looked through the glass. Heavily armed Iraqis beside great towers of poured-concrete blast walls regarded us sourly as we passed. At some checkpoints, they used a bullshit divining rod to see whether our car had explosives. (I'd later learn that it was manufactured by a single British shyster who'd bilked governments all over the Middle East and South Asia for millions. The device looked like a spray gun with a radio's antennae stapled to the bottle.)

On one vast blast wall surrounding Camp Victory—a sprawling U.S. military base—we saw the faint outline of a mural, but whatever it depicted was obscured entirely by brown mud. Shrubbery and stunted trees sagged with dirt and the Tigris flowed like a warm chocolate milkshake.

We shared the streets with Iraqi Humvees and armored personnel carriers, which looked worn-down and tiny next to the new generation of gigantic American war machines, the massive mine-resistant MRAPs, which drove fast and sported powerful gun turrets that, with their quick, rotating movements, seemed like impossibly large insects from some violent brown planet.

Kelly's U.S. military badge, which had taken her months to get, granted us access to the International Zone: the vast walled campus once known as the Green Zone and still home to the U.S. Embassy and the Iraqi parliament and other governmental institutions.

Anyone entering the IZ was a suspect. At one stop a German shepherd lunged at our truck, tugging at the chain, and I imagined I could smell the dog's meaty breath.

We pulled up to the place my wife called home. Along with reporters from several other news organizations, she shared a sprawling two-story villa, rented from an exile who lived in Jordan. It was on a walled-in street, and with a garden of grass and flowers in full bloom, it became our own personal IZ. I wheeled my luggage into the house and had a look around. In the vast kitchen—two ovens! two sinks!—we made coffee.

Sipping at hot cups, we were joined by some of Kelly's Iraqi colleagues—including the driver, Ahmed, who also was the office manager—plus several translators and other employees. One asked me how I liked Baghdad.

"I've only been here a few hours," I said.

"That's why we're asking you now," he said. He was thin, with sad eyes and a sparse head of hair. Kelly told me later he was an excellent reporter. He lived in two rooms with his parents, his wife, and his three children—forced out of their much larger house near the airport for being Shiites.

Up on the roof, smoking cigarettes under a hot sun, we heard and felt twin explosions in the distance. Kelly told me that if they were car bombs we would see a big column of black smoke. I searched the sky but saw only helicopters and brown haze. These were dull booms, she said. Probably just a round of mortars fired at the IZ.

Lunch at the house was a communal affair, with myself, Kelly, Muthana, Ahmed, and several other men on staff heaping plates with chicken and rice. We fought over sweet honey and nut pastries. I could still hear the helicopters, and I felt guilty, eating delicious things, safe behind the wall, free and even encouraged by these men to pass some judgment. But I was also excited and honored—overwhelmed, really—to be standing in the middle of it, hoping the darker forces of death and destruction would keep their distance and that my own enthusiasm to learn more, to believe that—with Kelly's ability to report well and to stay alive, with the resilience of the Iraqi people, with America's ability to be honest about its power and priorities, with my ability to have faith in something it was difficult to have faith in—maybe things might actually get better. By now, however, being an American in Iraq felt like the punch line to a joke.

It was 2010. All I could reasonably hope for was that that my trip wasn't a miscalculation, that I wasn't another bozo searching for an answer to a set of questions that shouldn't have ever been asked in the first place.

Blood pounding, I ate a date—freshly picked by the cook—and in awe, I found it still warm from the sun.

The Bank of Baghdad was located in the Al-Hamra Hotel, in a neighborhood previously home to many of the foreign journalists before a deadly car bombing the previous January. The explosion left mangled bodies, destroyed buildings, and an exposed crater in the ground reported to be a dozen feet wide and six feet deep. It had been one of three coordinated blasts targeting hotels that day. Nearly forty Iraqis died, and scores more were wounded.

Because of the bombing, changes had been made to Kelly's security policy, which was an ever-evolving portfolio of strategies. As such, we traveled to the bank in the armored truck, followed by a "soft car"—in this case a late-model Peugeot sedan, which could provide us cover and escape if anything crazy happened. Crawling through the dust-covered neighborhood, we nosed slowly around deep ruts or sped past idling cars containing unknown men.

Past a final checkpoint, we parked in the street and climbed the stairs to the hotel's lobby, where red-eyed men welcomed us laconically. The pool stood empty and brown. I tried to picture various reporters I knew here. Back in 2003, they would have been pink and authoritative, splayed out around the water in lounge chairs.

The bank office was a gloomy money cave, with three unsmiling women in tight head scarves sitting behind cluttered desks. We were in the bottom of the hotel's second tower, beside a set of the rooms ruined by the January bombing.

With Kelly and the tellers occupied, I explored the carnage, finding that in many cases workers had simply bricked in the parts of the building the blast had carved away. Roofing tiles hung askew and lights flickered. Behind a long-abandoned check-in desk was a yellowed newspaper entombed in ash. Mail addressed to people who may or may not have still been alive waiting in a few slots behind the desk. A stack of brittle paperback novels gathered dust.

Around the corner, a single bare bulb lit the partially ruined women's restroom, where pipes protruded from the ceiling. I wasn't sure there was running water, but it felt like an intimate transgression when I spotted a bar of soap and a tube of toothpaste. I flashed back to the women tellers and regretted what I'd seen. Behind the door to the men's restroom I found a dark pile of rubble as high as my shoulders. Where did the men go?

Then I found what I took to be the former hotel manager's office. A heavy layer of grime covered the desk. Rubble from the January bombing littered the shelves and an old office chair. I tried to picture an effusive, efficient Iraqi scrambling to please a hotel full of guests as American warplanes buzzed in the sky over his country. An empty coffee cup stood beside a pair of Iraqi flags mounted on a wooden dais. There was a ghostly set of handprints, as if someone had tried to sit in the chair one last time, then thought better of it. The scene was a workingman's life, frozen in time.

The next morning, at 6:30 AM, we awoke to the concussive boom of a nearby attack. Disoriented, I turned to Kelly, whose eyes were shut tight. How, I wondered, could she sleep through such a thing? Back in Istanbul I always worried that the sounds of the city would wake Loretta, but like her mother, the little girl slept through almost anything.

I closed my eyes and dreamed of explosions and dust. In the weak light of mid-morning, we went downstairs to drink coffee with the Iraqis, who told us they heard that one of the morning's rockets hit the nearby IZ, injuring two of the prime minister's guards. Another landed in the Tigris, and a third struck a building less than a mile from our bed, killing two civilians. I tried to imagine a mortar slamming into a river.

Kelly and I headed for the Tigris that night. Our hulking driver, Ahmed, gunned the engine around a long line of cars.

"We are VIP," he explained in Arabic to a lot attendant, and we ground gears in the heavy truck along a road that ran high above the swirling waters of the Tigris.

Sure, I was nervous at the prospect of a dinner among Iraqis. How many of the people I'd marched with back in New York had ever imagined eating dinner in Baghdad? I wouldn't begrudge an Iraqi if he took my dinner plate and slammed it into my face. I considered slamming a plate into my own face. I thought about Ahmed, who had called us important.

The restaurant was divided into a men-only section and a family section. There were sparsely grassed lawns with dozens of picnic tables on either side of a kitchen and a roaring open fire. We picked out a good table, and I assumed Ahmed would join us. But since a company vehicle had been blown up by a bomb placed underneath the car in 2008, Kelly told me that security policy required someone to stay with the truck. I watched him walk off into the dark.

The air next to the river was wet, and a spray of mosquitoes dined on our ankles. Families around us smoked shisha and picked at colorful salads. People laughed and talked animatedly. Some women wore tight clothing, flashing a bit of hair and shoulder. Others were head-to-toe in black.

It seemed unwise for us to be here, but equally crazy to cower in fear back at the house. I decided I was glad we'd gone out to dinner. After all, the Iraqis at the restaurant hadn't given up. (On this night, and so many others, Kelly hadn't either.) We held hands under the table.

The meal arrived. Carp had once been caught in the Tigris, but since that river had become both town dump and city morgue—and a place for rockets to fall—the fish were farm-raised. After a generous bath of lime and salt, they were set on their sides an arm's length from the fire. It took as long as an hour, but the slow roasting produced a crispy skin atop steaming, succulent meat. We ate heartily, tearing off pieces of fresh, hot bread.

Then a deep boom popped my ears. A mortar had landed, and I nearly fell out of my chair. An old Iraqi couple—amused by my reaction—allowed themselves thin smiles. Kelly laughed nervously.

"That was at least half a mile away," Kelly said.

"How nice," I said. "Think there'll be more?"

"Maybe."

We ate for a while in silence, then lit cigarettes. It was time to go, and I told Kelly I'd fetch Ahmed, who had the cash. Summiting the hill, I saw him as a dark figure, the red bead of a cigarette dancing as he gesticulated into his phone. He shook my hand, accepting my offer to watch the truck while he settled the bill.

Waiting, I paced the dark gravel. Then I heard shots. An Iraqi army patrol hit the lights on their Humvee. A pack of men headed toward me from the gloom. I searched for Ahmed—where was he?—and I didn't notice a man who'd split from the pack and was suddenly poking me in the chest, slurring in angry Arabic.

I met his wild eyes. He sputtered in frustration. I wasn't sure what to do. His crew stood there, ogling. If I tried to speak Arabic, they'd know I was a foreigner. If I stayed mum, he might hit me.

He looked at my eyes, and I noticed he'd missed a button on his shirt. I wanted to reach out and fix it, but I stopped myself. A gunshot rang out.

Then Ahmed and Kelly crunched up on the gravel and the guy scrambled away.

Ahmed cranked the truck to life and said the man was probably just *sakran*, Arabic for drunk. This spot by the river, he said, was one of the few places men could let off steam, which they did by drinking and firing guns.

I locked my door as we drove away.

On my last full day, I went with Kelly to the site of a massive car-bomb attack that had obliterated nearly half a city block several months earlier. The target was the local office of a Dubai-based, Saudi-funded TV station, whose reporting some perceived as in-sufficiently anti-American. En route to the scene, Kelly looked out the window and said the homemade bomb had killed four.

The carnage left me speechless. The sun beat down; this was the most daylight I had seen outside the car or company compound since I'd arrived. Kelly spoke in a mix of English and Arabic to a clutch of grim-faced army officials near the crater.

One of the hardest parts of coming to Iraq, I suppose, was knowing that I would soon be leaving Kelly behind. It's not like I'd never done this before. When we first started dating, I lived hours away and dreaded the moment each week when my bus would arrive to take me away. One of those beautiful fall days, when a sweater was enough but the air was crisp and bracing, Kelly stepped off the curb to cross the street. Just before she was hit by a speeding cab, filled with a strength and resolve I'd never before known that I possessed, I yanked her back. Leaving her in Baghdad was hard to deal with: Who'll yank her back when I'm not around?

A decade later, I walked the edges of this crater ringed with chipped rock and asphalt. The ball of flame had scorched a palm tree. I found half a belt, a pair of sunglasses broken in two, and a scarred sandal. The street was a mess of torn, blasted cars, every surface a burnt and battered witness to all that could go wrong in the world. I felt weak and outmatched.

Standing there in the bright sun, I knew I'd encountered a place that, as an American, I still had a burden to care deeply about, but one that—no matter how much emotion I brought forth, no matter how hard I tried—would resist my efforts to package or describe it. Despite any of our best efforts, it was a place that could just as easily become a place we'd all too happily forget.

Kicking at the rubble, I felt sweat pour down my neck and yearned to be far away.

Soon enough I'd be back with Loretta, the second person in my life I'd sworn to protect. For now, I regarded my wife, who stood in the shell of a collapsed building, arguing with a soldier. I watched her fingers squeeze into a white fist, saw her smile in frustration. It occurred to me that in such a male-dominated industry—almost always surrounded by Iraqi men or male Western colleagues—I might be the only one who noticed how long she'd let her nails grow.

For a time, she would live and work in Iraq, and I would have no choice but to trust that she would find her own balance, that she'd figure out how to care without caring too much, to give herself over as much as she could to the project of this caring without leading herself or others into harm, remaining a wife and a mother and the woman she wanted to be—and the war reporter she was quietly becoming.

I slipped a shard of twisted metal into my pocket.

BEHIND AN IRON DOOR

Kelly and I left our Spartan Riyadh hotel room, with its bouquet of sweat and sewage, to rendezvous with two American bankers we'd met at the Sharjah airport.

The bankers—one a buff guy with a buzz cut who looked like a parody of a CIA agent, the other a wry Korean American—picked us up, and off we barreled through snarls of sunbaked cars. Battle-scarred Crown Victorias gunned their engines past late-model Toyotas. A Hummer plowed over rumble strips, cutting off a brand-new 700-series BMW. The dust was thick. The low-slung immensity of central Riyadh—ten million people, economy booming on oil, population growing exponentially, housing at a premium—shimmered in the late summer heat.

This was home.

We were heading to the Diplomatic Quarter (or DQ), a sprawling, 1,600-acre compound that sat on Riyadh's western edge, the newest corner of the city. First, the bankers drove us past several half-erected mansions of the nouveau riche: one a nightmarish sheet cake of marble; another a monstrous, gabled cabin. The DQ security checkpoint was a more fearsome version of similar barriers all around the city, with machine-gun nests, swirling blue police lights, iron traffic spikes, and rolls of concertina wire. We pulled into the car park of Scalini's, an Italian restaurant. Inside, the bankers introduced us to the British manager of an English-language school. In the course of conversation, it became clear that the school had an empty apartment here—a fact that could change everything for us.

In 1902, King Abdul Aziz ibn Saud took Riyadh, rallying the country's tribes under one flag, and since then this harsh city on the high desert plateau had been the seat of Saudi government—at least in theory. But a brutal climate and a harsher manifestation of Islam than on either of the thickly settled east or west coasts of the country meant Riyadh long remained one of the most closed-off cities on earth. For years, most commerce and trade in Saudi Arabia took place in Jeddah, the Red Sea port town, which hosted the country's government ministries and foreign embassies in addition to many of its outward-looking private enterprises. (And just up the road from Jeddah were the two holiest sites in Islam—Mecca and Medina—to which millions of pilgrims streamed each year.). In 1975, however, it was announced that the foreign ministry and embassies would be moving to Riyadh, and with that, many of the westerners and Saudis would be moving too—some to an experimental new neighborhood: the DQ.

"You want to live here, huh?" the Briton asked, eyebrows raised and a sly smile stretched under his thin moustache. I thought about our dank little room back in town. We did want to live there, we wanted it badly.

In September 2008, three hundred families—diplomats, businessmen, foreigners and Saudis alike—were already on the waiting list for DQ apartments. People allegedly paid "key money" fees of as much as thirty-five thousand dollars to jump the queue. We didn't have that kind of money, and not to sound too naive and moralistic, but we refused to pay the bribe. The school manager said he might be able to help, and so we ate dinner and hoped.

Having glimpsed the fortified quiet, we tried our best to make do back in the city. Our room had a small kitchen, was a few blocks from a supermarket, and we watched a lot of CNN. We'd paid thirty days in advance.

Finally, a few days before our month was up, the mustachioed school manager called—he could meet me that afternoon. I hailed a taxi and two hours later I was standing in a sprawling, three-bedroom apartment, keys in hand. Delirious at our luck, I padded around the sea-green carpeting. Children had scrawled half-finished words on the walls in crayon. Each room had a few broken-down pieces of furniture. The TV didn't work. In the kitchen, a giant 1980s refrigerator rumbled as if powered by a diesel generator. But it was ours.

The DQ master plan had called for a mix of official buildings and housing for up to twenty thousand people, mostly diplomats and their support staff, with the remainder offered to other expats and Saudis. Reportedly, to build it had cost nearly a billion dollars. More than fifty kilometers of roads were paved, then lined with apartments and villas, parks and trails, mosques and shops. For their embassy buildings, countries were encouraged to embrace traditional Saudi Arabian architectural styles: a sandy color palette, crenellated rooftops, few windows, nothing higher than three or four stories.

I set out on foot the day we moved in for a grocery a mile away, walking down tree-lined boulevards, through elegant marble arches, and past a massive, glass-walled conference center; in fifteen minutes of walking, I didn't see a single car. After negotiating a series of empty terracotta squares with burbling fountains, I reached the store, which was closed for prayer. I sat on a bench and watched the wind kick up drifts of sand. The heavy wooden door creaked open nearly an hour later and I had to acknowledge that the cashier was the first person I'd seen outside my apartment all day. I returned three hours after I'd left, and all I had to show for it was a carton of milk and a wand of butter.

A few weeks passed and I felt more and more that I was living in a ghost town. With its wide avenues and spacious public squares, the DQ was designed to accommodate a daily stream of visitors. But this vision had been clouded by bomb attacks that Saudi extremists carried off within the city between 2003 and 2006, killing nearly two hundred civilians and soldiers. Westerners fled Riyadh; concrete barriers, tanks, and soldiers were posted around the city; in the remote outskirts, along the broad mesas and flats surrounding the DQ, the tires of military four-by-fours on patrol had worn deep grooves into the soft sand. In one night, Al Qaeda-linked militants stormed three different compounds—private versions of the DQ—going methodically from house to house shooting men, women, and children. A team detonated a car bomb packed with golf balls timed to strafe anyone who'd come out to see what was happening. The explosion tore through homes for blocks around. Entire companies closed up shop and sent their staff back home. Leaving the house became a frightening prospect. Few thought it was a fun activity to picnic anymore.

By the time we met the bankers and moved to Riyadh in 2008, the most recent bombing was years in the past, and thanks to the world economy's contraction, Riyadh was a more attractive posting than ever. At least according to the rental offices, the DQ was near full occupancy. But I could never find anybody.

Life was lived behind closed doors. Saudi had always embraced a tradition of secrecy and privacy, harkening back to tribal times. The country's embrace of the strictest interpretation of Islam constricted public life further. No woman would dare show her bare arms or hair, and Saudi was a place that cherished a closed door. Fearing the religious police (the bearded enforcers who roamed the capitol armed with canes and were invested with religious authority), Westerners in Saudi had plenty of reason not to challenge the norm.

Desperate for air, I started jogging at night on a sandy trail that meandered along the reinforced perimeter of the DQ. Once, under a full moon, I encountered a half-dozen big-eared, long-tailed foxes. Another night, Kelly told me she'd seen a light burning at the bombed-out farmer's house just over the security fence, which stretched for dozens of mostly unguarded kilometers. Across the city people were still spooked by the threat of Al Qaeda violence; every new building had a blast wall and razor wire and guys with guns. How easily, I wondered, could someone sneak under the wire? While I was nostalgic for the DQ's picnicking past—a past I'd never know—I was grateful for our apartment's blast-proof iron front door.

WITHOUT CHIEF OR TRIBE

I was having lunch at the swan near Hyde Park and *some son of a bitch took my bag with all my documents*, the email began. It was June of 2009 and I was sitting at a desk in Riyadh. Assuming this was spam, I was about to press delete, when something made me reconsider.

Outside, it was summer in Saudi, where temperatures could exceed one hundred and thirty degrees. Kelly and I had lived in the country for nearly a year. We'd spent much of our lives in foreign countries or in strange corners of North America. We'd met in Cambodia, spent years in Southeast Asia, got to know Russia and the former Soviet Union, and I proposed to her on a fishing boat in Alaska. This time, however, the Middle East in general seemed a little beyond my talent set. Maybe it was the heat making me feel weak? By this time of year everyone was spending entire days indoors, emerging only to drive air-conditioned cars, in which metal could be so hot it might burn your skin. Streets buckled, the wind howled in from the desert, and meanwhile booze was still illegal, women were forbidden from consorting with men they weren't related to, and it was hard to imagine why anyone would ever choose to settle here. Considering all this, we—the swashbuckling couple who had never shied away from doing something insane—were about to bring a new baby into the world.

Earlier that spring, my wife had consulted with our doctor, who was open to natural birth. Pressed, she admitted that even at this, the best hospital in the country, we couldn't know in advance which doctor we might get for the actual event. Most doctors, we feared, would just wheel in the knives and proceed to surgery. In Saudi Arabia, women could have up to eight babies, and the rich ones understandably came to view childbirth with as much ceremony as a hair appointment and scheduled caesareans weeks in advance. After these procedures, the nurse would arrive, take the baby to the nursery, and when it was time to leave, a nanny fed the child and carried her to the car. Honestly, I didn't think that sounded too bad. And Kelly might have agreed, too, had we not met that Swiss doula at a camel race outside town. While we watched the beasts galumph around a desert oval, the beatifically maternal Swiss woman advocated for a natural birth with as little to do with medicine or surgery as possible. Over the next few days, driving around Riyadh's wind-blown terrain, we talked and I suppose both became convinced—enamored, really, by the challenge of it. After all, it seemed ironic—in an otherwise throwback culture, which was leery of modern progress, which loved all things pure and holy—that they might consider a natural birth odd and subversive. Kelly heard about a doctor who could help. We drove to his clinic with a stack of cash nearly half an inch thick. The money—five thousand dollars—was a guarantee he'd come any time, day or night, no matter what.

"Don't worry," he said after we'd paid the receptionist. "I'll be there when you need me."

Driving home, I remember thinking how easy that had been, but also what kind of freedom we'd lost in the transaction. Already, we were beginning to accumulate things that might slow us down. The rental car was about six hundred dollars a month. After we were kicked out of our semi-legal crash pad in the DQ, we took a risk and rented a roach-infested apartment in the middle of the city beside the Kuwaiti souk. Almost everyone in the building was a deeply religious Saudi family. But what could we do? We'd soon be parents and needed a place to stay. The landlord required all six months up front, an amount that would get you a month in a sprawling penthouse in Manhattan. We were paying all that in one of the harshest climates in the world, in the country perhaps more hostile to outsiders than any other, where Islam was practiced in its strictest form, where people were executed for witchcraft and adultery. We were incredibly alone and trying to have a baby in a country where family and religion was sacred, where the locals were intensely loyal to whatever group or ideas they considered theirs, and where rising oil prices meant everyone was getting rich. Meanwhile, we were living on the edge, without tribe or chief, attempting to ask questions of ourselves and others and be open to the world, making it as freelance writers without health insurance or savings, no real safety net, and no formal support except for the distant and somewhat restrained awe and encouragement of friends and family back home. ("You live where? Why?") Now we thought it'd be a good idea to become parents.

Occasionally, thinking about the implications of becoming a dad, I wondered if I'd ever again do something like walk from New York to New Orleans, which I'd done in 2007. All of a sudden, I had a pregnant wife and drove through hellish traffic in a city of ten million people, in the middle of the desert, and I'd recall how it was only on the slimmest of pretexts—a new kind of journalist visa—that we'd even been admitted to Saudi Arabia in the first place. For decades prior, few Western reporters had been allowed much more than a short visit, during which they would be clung to by a government minder. But when the Saudi ambassador in Washington, impressed as he was that she occasionally worked for NPR, offered Kelly a week's visa—and later when he agreed to sponsor me, though not to work, just as a spouse—we jumped at the chance. Who could say no to the opportunity to access one of the most under-covered and misunderstood corners of the world? Well, perhaps a lot of people. But not us. We could not say no.

When our 747 landed in September 2008 and we cleared passport control, we couldn't believe our luck that no minder appeared, that we could simply retrieve our bags, walk out into the fearsome heat, flag down a taxi, and do whatever and go wherever we chose. It felt like everything was snapping into place.

That first night we went to the cheapest hotel in town. Moving from crap room to crap room, we managed, with some haggling over money and rules, to replace our original weeklong visas with a month's permission, later converted into a three-month permit. We felt cocky, I suppose. Then Kelly learned she was pregnant. We attended a party that week with a bunch of diplomats, and I sipped their illicit champagne as we talked feverishly about what to do next. For the first time we envied, rather than ridiculed, the various British accents and networks of support and jobs and health care everyone was plugged into. Untethered from a world of parents and friends—the people you might take for granted when you're wild and young, but the community that feels so critical when you're pregnant—we wondered: Should we go home? I downed another glass, and we decided, fuck it, let's do this.

That winter we secured a pair of six-month permissions. Kelly was already four months pregnant. If everything went well, she'd give birth in June and we'd get out just before our visas expired. (If you overstayed your visa, you could be deported, imprisoned, or worse.)

Her belly got bigger, and I started writing more regularly, and she filed reports for NPR. When she was at full term, our visas were set to expire, and the due date was just a few days before my thirtieth birthday. Both of our moms were flying in to help—mine first, to be replaced immediately thereafter by Claudia, Kelly's mom. With all of this on my mind, I sat at my computer in what would eventually be our daughter's room, preparing to work on a book I'd been attempting to write for several years, trying to cool off when I opened the email that would change the tenor of what was already a complicated couple of weeks.

I was having lunch at the swan near Hyde Park and some son of a bitch took my bag with all my documents. The email was riddled with bizarre but authentic-feeling typos. *It is sunday—US consulate closed til tomorrow...there are copies of my visa and passport on the frig \9\i cannot remember Al's email address-phone is almost dead-\i have nothing!!! what to do now...*

Al: That was my father's name. This wasn't spam. My mom was stranded in London hours before I was to pick her up at the airport in Riyadh, days before my wife was to go into labor.

Working illegally, I'd recently been let go from one crappy media job, and inexplicably lucked into a second crappy media job at the last minute. The boss at the new shop agreed it wouldn't make sense for me to start working while my wife was in labor. I could start, we agreed, a day or two after my kid's birth.

The whole situation was a bit overwhelming. I tried not to think about how badly we needed the money. Then there was or the fact that my mom was stranded in London. With a brain frying from the high heat of an Arabian summer, I couldn't help thinking again of the several thousand dollars we might need if there were complications—plus enough to pay for rent, to buy a bed before my mom arrived—if she ever did—and still more to host Kelly's mom, Claudia, who would arrive as my mom departed. Could you put a C-section on a credit card? I hoped you could. I slapped myself. I stopped stressing and I started writing.

Dear Clive Ward, I began, responding to the unfamiliar email address. *Are you my mom?*

Clive Ward, it turned out, was my mom's new friend and the manager of the Hyde Park Hotel. During a ten-hour layover, she'd left Heathrow and taken the Tube to Hyde Park. At a nearby pub, her purse had been stolen along with her wallet, passport, and brand-new camera. When I finally talked to the woman who'd given birth to me, her voice was shaky, and she expressed a great deal of regret about going to the pub. I calmed her down as best as I could and walked her through what she'd do: Get an emergency AmEx card, withdraw a bunch of cash, go to the US embassy for a new passport, beg the Saudi consulate in London for a new visa. This kind of stuff was old hat for Kelly and I, but it felt like a lot to put my mom through, and I began to think that maybe we'd overextended ourselves.

Bright and early Monday morning, with a fistful of cash and a new credit card, my mom waited at the US Embassy only to have American officials cheerfully inform her that the passport photos she'd gotten were a tad too small. She'd need to go make new ones. In tears, she wandered nearby streets trying to find a place that could make photos the right size for America.

The next day, with a new U.S. passport in hand, she asked the Saudi Embassy if they'd reissue her lost visa, without which she'd be turned away at the airport in Riyadh. It seemed like a simple request—especially with the backing of the Ambassador in DC—but London officials said, with regret, that it was in fact only the Saudi Embassy *in the U.S.* that could reissue such permission. Kelly's due date was Thursday.

Miraculously, my mom arrived before the baby. On the day Kelly was due, with no signs yet of labor, I took the ladies to an Indian restaurant in Riyadh, where modesty laws required that we all sit in a booth behind a curtain, so that no one could see my wife or my mom's faces. To summon a waiter, there was a button in the middle of the table. Whenever he arrived to bring more naan or to refresh our water, the waiter avoided our gaze. We ordered the spiciest food on the menu, hoping it might induce Kelly's labor. My mom tried to be of good cheer. She was totally exhausted. London had cost her at least a thousand dollars. She needed a drink, but with Saudi's strict rules against alcohol, we'd be lucky to have even a small taste of booze while she was here.

After lunch, we went to the mall. Other than mosques and a handful of grim parks, it was the only place in the entire city we could relax outside the apartment. (Movie theaters were outlawed; public space in general was highly charged and patrolled by religious police, who carried clubs.) Under the fluorescent glow, Kelly drank from a quart bottle of pineapple juice—said also to help induce labor—and she rode the escalator down, then walked up the stairs, repeating this over and over in hopes of jostling our child into being.

Every time we left the house I braced myself for some strange experience: Religious police asking us for our marriage license, a car wreck in which I might have to pay blood money, or an eager proselytizer trying to convert my family to Islam. With my slow-moving wife an easy target, I expected we might be accosted by a crowd of horny teenagers. I scanned the area. One afternoon, in the same mall, I'd seen a boy on an ATV ride in through the glass doors, rev his engine around the courtyard, and blast back outside, gunning his machine into traffic. There wasn't much to do here.

The next night, my birthday, Kelly's water broke. The contractions started rolling in, and we cracked a bottle of white wine a diplomat gave us. My mom and I sipped, taking turns napping. Eventually, Kelly began to moan from the pain, but still she was adamant about not going to the hospital before she was ready. For two hours, she sat in the bathroom, the only spot in the house she felt comfortable, all the while moaning and slumping over. When she finally agreed to go, it was four in the morning. She'd been in labor for seven hours, and she could barely talk, let alone walk.

It took us an hour to get her pants on, then my mom and I frog-marched her into the car, where she was laid out like some kind of injured mermaid, sprawling in pain across the front passenger seat, which I'd reclined to full capacity. By that time of the night, the desert air had cooled. A light breeze ruffled a few palms. No cars were out, and you could hear the click of the traffic lights as they changed colors. The baby seat we'd bought for the occasion was in the trunk, as were snacks and water and various bags of gear. The car roared to life and I started driving northeast, through the city's sprawling outer developments. Billboards advertised imported soup, luxury cars, and washing machines. I floored it between speed bumps, which, when hit, caused Kelly to groan. The hospital was twenty minutes away. Could I deliver a baby by the side of the road? I drove as fast as I could.

At last, I could see the emblem of the hospital—the outline of a palm beside a crescent moon—and at sixty miles per hour I barreled into the parking lot. A male attendant watched with wide eyes as Kelly limped in the door. Nurses examined her. She was already dilated eight centimeters.

The team that morning included women from Jordan and Tunisia. I'd met the Jordanian earlier in the week, when we'd dropped off a box of sweets along with the latest copy of our birth plan. I'd felt foolish then, but seeing familiar faces, I was glad we'd taken the time. My mom unpacked our bags, and I thought someone might object when she set up speakers that quietly played hippie flute music. Then she hung some eagle feathers on a wall, and our room began to feel like some sort of Ashram—illegal in a country that banned all religion but Islam—and for a second I thought about what might go wrong.

Soon, we were hurtling toward the final push. I checked my watch. The doctor we'd paid all that money to still wasn't here. I asked one of the nurses, and she shrugged. That's when I noticed the appearance of another doctor, covered head to toe in a fearsome, strangely form-fitting Islamic robe, which revealed only her eyes—she was even wearing black gloves—making her look like a severe little ninja. Behind her came an orderly, who was wheeling in a cart of gleaming surgical equipment. This was exactly what we didn't want to happen.

The tiny doctor lifted up Kelly's robe, and her hand disappeared under the fabric. My wife began to bellow. She'd hunted for pirates in Indonesia, nearly had her arm torn off when we worked on a fishing boat in Alaska, and a few years from this moment, she'd embed with Syrian rebels. In this hospital on this day, her face was ashen and furious. I worried she might kill this tiny doctor. Taking care not to touch the black-robed woman, I ushered the doctor out of the room, explaining that we'd already paid for a specialist to be in attendance, that he was in fact en route (I hoped), that our birth plan requested no drugs or any major intervention unless absolutely necessary, that this plan was posted to the wall in the nurse's station, that under no circumstances was she to come back into our room for any reason. She clicked her tongue at me and walked away. Kelly, grunting, took refuge in the bathroom.

I stood outside the door, listening. There was a low moan. I went in.

"Just give me some gas," she pleaded. "Just a little? Pleeeeeee-ase. I need it."

We'd practiced this. Kelly wanted to do the birth without drugs. In the moment, we were told it was all but certain she'd want them. Yet she'd ordered me not to listen to her begging or reasoning. I was to do whatever it took not to let her have what she wanted.

"They don't have any," I said, hoping she'd forgive me. "They're all out."

So fragile was Kelly—who normally took no shit—that she simply looked at me sadly, eyes wide, believing me completely. It was hard to imagine any other situation in which she'd take no for an answer.

My mom edged into the bathroom with a cup of Gatorade. The doctor had finally arrived. I poured some of the red stuff into Kelly's mouth, as if she were a bird, taking care not to bump her nose. She hung her head, having neither eaten nor consumed liquid in twelve hours. As I hugged her shoulders, I felt her muscles liven, fortified perhaps by the salts and sugar. With a sigh, she let me help lift her off the toilet. Her head fell on my shoulder. She wore a loose gown and her skin was warm. I held her arm and walked her slowly through the door. She looked at me, climbed slowly up onto the bed. Then she got into position.

For that last hour—or was it five minutes?—I sat on the bed behind her, my legs out, steadying her, sometimes rubbing her back. My thighs cramped up so badly they'd felt like they might explode. Solidarity, I thought. But whatever I felt was nothing. I listened to all kinds of strange noises, and all I could see was the face of the Jordanian nurse, who smelled like cigarettes.

"Let's go," she said to Kelly, speaking in Arabic. "Let's go, honey. Let's go, let's go."

Just after eight AM, I scrambled off the bed, putting my hand to our baby's chest, saying, "Hello, baby, it's so nice to meet you," keeping contact as the doctor moved the two of us across the room to a small theater—me chanting, "Hey, baby. I'm here. Honey, I'm here"—when the doctor proceeded to look for signs of life. Seeing the little swollen bits between a tiny set of legs, my mom screamed, "It's a boy!"

But she wasn't. This was Loretta, who with one final thwack against her chest cried. I lifted her up, placed her on Kelly's chest, and nearly fell to the ground in triumph. My birthday was over.

A day later, I sat in the hushed office of my new employer, a Lebanese-Syrian publishing company, which had postponed my start date until Loretta was born. The boss was agreeable enough—offering a congratulatory slice of his pizza and a few bites of his salad—but I'd soon learn that he was always too busy, preoccupied with making another deal. He had no time to oversee any of the projects he'd already agreed to. Plus, it was so difficult to recruit and train anyone to work in Saudi Arabia. His crew was a mix of weirdoes—the desperate, the incompetent, and the insane. In the sleepless haze of post-birth, I fit in just fine.

Most of my colleagues hunched unhappily behind ancient computers, tapping away at whatever it was I could never figure out, biding time before the next trip home. One guy was completely cross-eyed. Another seemed to speak no recognizable language.

But they all presumably had families they loved as much as I loved my own. However alienating Riyadh was for all of us, each of us had a connection as strong as the one I felt to two people back at an apartment across town. The only woman on staff was pregnant.

Unlike in less-wealthy Oman or Yemen, Saudi Arabia's staggering oil profits were distributed in such a way that few nationals did much work. Foreign workers were imported to staff restaurants and shops, to build roads and fix and install technology, to manage and grow the thriving commercial sector. It wasn't easy to get someone to come here from abroad. Whether they sought a janitor or a graphic designer or a writer, companies had to pay for annual flights back, and most firms even supplied housing.

A majority of those Saudis who did work had cushy jobs in state agencies paid for by oil profits where they were reported to drink lots of tea. But a new law on the books required private enterprise to employ at least one local. Ours was a handsome dude in his early twenties who arrived at ten AM in his red sports car. Most days, he'd glide into the office, take off his sunglasses, listen to a little music, surf the web, make some tea, then go home. One day I asked him to translate some stuff for an article I was writing about Japan. He looked at me quizzically then wandered off to the bathroom.

We met regularly with clients, piling into the CEO's luxury sport utility vehicle, plowing down kilometers of new asphalt, where we'd arrive at the gleaming headquarters of some massive state-run medical cooperative or an oil conglomerations. Our sales pitch was to produce a variety of unreadable magazines and in-house circulars or occasionally a glossy brochure for a company who sold specialty drill bits or plastic sacks for transporting salt. I wore rumpled dress shirts and tried to smile. My role was to be the marginally enthusiastic American, trotted out to speak perfect English and say a few words of encouragement, such as, "We care about your company's success" or "I love health care and corporate social responsibility in equal measure," justifying, I suppose, whatever huge fees we were charging. The whole thing was demoralizing at times but always fascinating and occasionally hilarious. When we met up with friends—many of them diplomats or journalists—I never told anyone where I worked, because it was all technically illegal, seeing as how I was in the country as the spouse of a journalist. And I was also embarrassed. On my worst days, I told myself this: Enjoy the money and think of the whole thing as a crazy experiment.

More importantly, there was the matter of an exit visa for Loretta. Until she had some kind of Saudi paperwork, we learned, there'd be no attempting to leave the country. In essence, according to local jurisprudence, Loretta wasn't even ours. My mom was long gone and Claudia had only stayed for two weeks. We spent much of their visits lying around in a giant bed, watching baby TV. Since Loretta's birth, Kelly had stayed home, breast-feeding and cooing. And though she had done all the work to put things in motion, it was I who chipped away at the mountain of paperwork required to get us out of the country. On short lunch breaks, when I wasn't cutting out of work early to go to some obscure office to get a new stamp or form, I would cross an eight-lane highway thick with Suburbans driven by crazed teenagers in order to pace the halls of a mostly moribund mall near my office. I'd smoke cigarettes and drink Diet Pepsi, and in a way that was becoming all too familiar, I couldn't stop thinking about all the things that could go wrong.

First we needed a Saudi birth certificate, which required U.S. embassy–approved translations and notarizations. With those in hand, plus several forms printed out and filled out in triplicate, plus a bunch of photos of Loretta, who when taken to a photo studio was two days old and asleep, only then could I get in line at the U.S. embassy to get her a passport, which had to be manufactured in the United States and sent back to Saudi. Disclaimers in all caps from the State Department warned us that they couldn't help us if we overstayed our visa, that jail time was possible, that heads of families had indeed been forced to send their children home while they battled some immigration case. Waiting in line to pick up the passport one afternoon, I watched as a woman sobbed, "I want my husband. Where is my husband? Can't someone help me!" With time running out, I drove to the dreaded immigration headquarters in south Riyadh, where I would submit the U.S. documents along with several inscrutable Arabic papers I could not even begin to decipher. It was a mind-meltingly sunny day in July, and I was waiting in an epic line when a man slithered up beside me like an eel. His teeth were bad and he seemed drunk.

"I can help you fill out your forms," he said.

A roomful of men turned to look at us.

"I'm okay," I said. But I wasn't.

Years before, I might have figured out how to enjoy this, or at least see it as a bit of an adventure. But with the stakes so high— Loretta was so small!—I couldn't help jumping to conclusions.

What if they tried to take her away from us? She was born on their soil, and we were at their mercy. The consequences of failure were of a magnitude so vast and incomprehensible that I couldn't stomach any kind of problem. When I was twenty-four and living in Indonesia, for instance, the prospect of going to jail was kind of hilarious. But as a father, there was nothing to laugh at, just the little girl who needed me to complete her paperwork.

Through the window I saw a line of what looked like Afghan guest workers outside. Their legs were chained to a long iron rod, and they shuffled in the sun across a sandy lot. My shirt was soaked through and I imagined my own legs in chains and then my ladies in limbo and I couldn't take it anymore and—I'm not proud of this—I skipped ahead of all the men from Bangladesh and Sri Lanka and India and walked right to the front desk.

"You have to help me," I said, pleading, staring into the eyes of a very thin Saudi army colonel in epaulets who was smoking a cigarette. He took a long drag. "My daughter," I said, showing him a picture. "We need to get her home in time for an important religious ceremony."

This was our trump card: baptism. I hadn't been to church voluntarily in my entire life, but Kelly's grandmother had long worked in a convent, where Kelly's aunt was still a nun. My grandmother on my dad's side prayed for us all the time. For all of them, we'd decided to give the little girl her dunk in the holy water.

The man put down his cigarette. Religion meant something here, even if wasn't Islam; faith commanded respect, and more importantly, action. He walked to a shelf filled with thick leather binders. Paging through the yellowing paper of one, he found an open space and took out an ink pen. Peering closely at my shaky handwriting and the picture of our newborn daughter, he slowly began to write. Then he stopped, inspected my forms again. I held my breath. I said a little prayer. Was something wrong? Then with a sigh, he resumed scratching, producing line after line of flowing Arabic. Finally, he took out a stamp, moistened it with a small sponge, affixed it to little Loretta's passport page, signed, and with that, we could leave.

Back in America, Loretta was baptized, and we began a sort of victory tour up and down the East Coast. In New York, we grilled pork sausages and clinked cold beers. On a sunny day in Miami, where my parents lived, I watched my dad hold his squirming grandchild. It felt like nothing could go wrong.

Then, NPR, which had been flirting with giving Kelly a better gig, issued fresh signals that a full-time correspondent job might be in the cards. With more to prove—to ourselves and others—we went back to Saudi Arabia.

We were on a short assignment in Yemen months later when we learned my dad was sick. By the time I got to the hospital in Florida, where he died, I realized how tired I was. A few weeks later, after another lunch in D.C., NPR made Kelly an offer she couldn't refuse.

Sitting on a lawn in suburban Virginia, my dad dead and buried, I talked to my wife on the phone minutes after she'd accepted the job. My daughter picked at pieces of tender grass. In some ways, we would finally have the stability a new child seemed to demand. The problem was that Kelly's new job was in Baghdad.

THE CHEST OF THE HORSE

For several months before we left Saudi Arabia, I dodged phone calls from our new landlord, avoiding an invitation to his farm in the remote north of Riyadh. Why was I afraid? In part, I couldn't get excited about taking our newborn deep into the desert. But at a certain point to decline his invitation would be too much disrespect. It was a mild day, perfect for a little trip. Kelly and I loaded up our rented Toyota. We carried blankets and plush toys and water and food, and with our daughter asleep in her car seat, we drove north.

The miles clicked by, and I scanned the road for a sign in Arabic reading EXIT FOUR. It wasn't clear how far we'd need to go, and with the brown earth stretching endlessly, the gas meter sinking, and the sound of our tires slapping against the pavement, I fought off a mounting feeling of dread by telling Kelly what I knew of our host.

I'd come to know Mohammad gradually, first as we negotiated the rental price for the 1980s unit in Central Riyadh, which was dark but roomy and situated in a deeply conservative neighborhood where everyone hid from each other. Then he and I spent an afternoon together on an appliance-purchasing trip, arguing over whether to buy a gas or electric stove. In a gesture that made me swell with pride—an actual Saudi was inviting me to hang out!—he later asked me to his family's *istriha,* a sort of meeting house .When we got there, however, the place was cold and empty. He showed me vast rooms that on other occasions might have been filled with family and festivity. Tonight, it was just us. He took two plastic chairs outside. We sat by a dark pool and I shivered in the cold wind.

"You know any good jokes?" he said. He told me how his old Romanian friend knew lots of good dirty ones—wink, wink—and that he could reliably get bottles of booze pilfered from the Embassy. We sipped warm Pepsi. Mohammed lit a new Marlboro Light off his expiring Marlboro Light.

Walking me to my car, he told me that he had been born in 1963, one of twelve sons of an upper-class family. He'd attended junior high in Los Angeles while his father was studying in America. After graduating from a Saudi high school, he began working for Sabic, the sprawling Saudi petroleum and plastics company. He started in the warehouse, rose steadily through the ranks, and eventually was sent by the company to study at Boston University. Upon his return, he did well enough that he could retire in his forties and move his wife and children from their dark apartment (where we now lived) into a Riyadh mini-mansion. He patted the top of my car, telling me he had a farm in the desert.

"You should visit," he said. "It will be nice."

Exit Four looped up and over a bridge. I could see nothing except the undulating hills of sand. Kelly asked if we were close. I pulled over and in the distance we could see the faint outline of a Toyota pickup—a Jihadi Mobile, as people called them. It sped toward us, kicking up an after-burn of fine sand.

Then my phone rang. I picked it up.

"Is it you?" Mohammad purred. "Follow me."

Soon the asphalt broke apart and it was just dirt. Our tiny sedan bounced over rocks and slammed into ruts. Loretta stirred, yawning.

When we had first met to negotiate rent for the apartment, Mohammad whipped out a giant cell phone to show me grainy photos of the new dream house. Just as he'd finished erecting the place, he explained, a flash flood had struck. I saw in several snapshots that a great river of mud had knocked over palms, threaded fissures into retaining walls, and filled his pool with brown slurry.

"You'll see when you visit," he said. "You'll love my castle."

We rounded the bend and it came into focus: a three-story sand-colored house with a moat, scalloped walls, and acres of desert. We parked on an insanely steep driveway that had probably made more sense on paper. I slowly picked up Loretta, who was still asleep in her car seat, and laid her beside a plastic table on a concrete patio. I put another blanket over her and Mohammad encouraged us to get comfortable. He took long drags on a five-foot shisha. He drank a homemade concoction of dark purple hooch and motioned to a stack of cups, inviting us to join him. From his laconic movements, I could tell it wasn't his first glass.

There wasn't another human being for miles. We admired the view, and Mohammed began explaining how there had been a battle centuries ago right on the spot where we were sitting

"Just after the Prophet's time," he said. The people had been outnumbered. But the tribe's fiercest warrior did not hesitate. He rode his beast directly into the enemy. Spears pierced his steed, Mohammad told us, but the leader pushed on.

"I call my land the——" Mohammad paused, frustrated. "You know, it is the horse. The breast of the horse." He pointed to his chest.

"The chest of the horse?" I said.

"Yes, that is the one."

I winced, thinking of a struggling animal riddled by sharp points.

Then Mohammad brightened, pulled out his wallet, and laid a well-worn ID card on the table. Kelly picked it up.

"Nice mustache," she said.

It was Mohammad's Boston University ID, dated 1984-1985. His kids sometimes wanted to play with it, Mohammad told us, but wary of the card fraying, he wouldn't let them anymore.

"I hate this fucking country," he said, sitting back in his chair.

Lately, he confided, it was his kids that caused him the most angst. He was happily married, but his wife's brothers were more conservative than Mohammad. "They take my kids and enroll them in summer school," he said. "When they come back, they talk like little Bin Ladens. It's bullshit."

Loretta began to cry. Kelly needed to breast feed and asked if there was a room inside.

"Yes, of course," Mohammad said, leading us through the kitchen, where the box for a fridge was still in a corner. Space for a stove was empty and raw. In a front room were windows covered with blackout tape. Kelly sat on a red carpet.

"You'll be okay?" I said.

"Sure," Kelly said slowly. "Why don't you go outside."

I couldn't make out the expression on her face.

I climbed into Mohammad's truck, and we drove at an astonishing speed, bouncing over gullies and racing around corners. I was surprised to see Mohammad was actually farming the land: rows of palms stood beside a thirty-foot plot of peppers, spring onions, and eggplants.

"Your wife and kids ever come here?" I asked.

Mohammed shook his head. He was concentrating on driving through a moonscape of rock and fossilized sea creatures.

"When did Columbus discover America?" he asked—growing serious as he punched the gas, waiting for my answer.

"In 1492," I said reflexively, nearly in singsong, wondering how far we were going.

"This place is much older than that," Mohammad said. He tapped the steering wheel and we jerked to a stop.

In the middle of this blank desert were the remains of an ancient village. Sand and mud walls stretched some twenty feet high. It was exhilarating to find the remains of a three-story guard tower. I fingered the rough walls. The constant assault of time and wind had revealed the stones that made the wall strong. It was rare to find anything so old in Saudi Arabia. Anything that did not glorify Islam or signal the country's emergence as a modern state was often destroyed. Mohammad offered to take photos, but the offer felt obligatory. He looked at his watch, ready to go. I imagined how easily he—or his brother-in-law—could demolish all this.

Back at the house, we found Kelly sitting alone. Loretta was inside, asleep. She gave me a look and I told Mohammad we'd probably need to leave soon.

"Stay as long as you want," he said. "I'm not going to kidnap you."

He went for another cup of homemade hooch.

"Take some," he said, filling a tall cup.

"No, thanks," Kelly said.

Mohammad sat back in his chair.

The fire had gone out and he jumped up to get it going. Once the fire roared, he took some pieces of marinated chicken from a foil packet. The meat sizzled on a wire rack and Mohammad plucked out a piece of burning coal with a pair of tweezers.

"Next time, you must bring your friends," he said.

He tossed the coal back into the fire.

The sun was going down and it was cold. We ate some of the food.

"I want to show you something," he said.

I followed him inside, happy to be up and moving about. We snaked through empty rooms. A bare bulb lit a hallway that led to a set of stairs. I saw Mohammed take quick steps and followed. Down a dark hallway, there was a room brightened only by the light of the moon. In the corner was a tall closet, and I watched as he reached up, searching for something.

When he turned around, he was holding a small, gray pistol.

My heart raced as he began to pace the room, turning his arm one way and then the other. Downstairs, he had seemed slow moving or sad, but now his body had a quickness to it that broadcast strength and resolve. Then he stopped, holding the gun, and I didn't like the tightness of the grip, or his finger's position on the trigger.

"You can put it back," I said. "I've seen it—you don't need to show me anything more."

"Don't worry," he said, leveling the pistol at the window, the metal shining in the moonlight. "It's not loaded. I just want to show it to you."

I braced myself, waiting for the blast, the shattering of glass, my wife's scream, our daughter's cry. Mohammad turned and smiled.

Suddenly he started stealing back downstairs, the white fabric of his long flowing thobe swished as he raced toward Kelly.

"She hates guns," I said, dashing after him. "Please don't do this!" I heard him say, as if in a trance: "This is my Spanish pistol."

"How nice," Kelly said, holding Loretta. She smiled through clenched teeth.

Out of breath, I gave her a wild look, deciding the best thing I could do was to take my landlord's arm and steer him away.

"It's not loaded," he said to me, quietly, as we walked together out into the desert night. He pulled the trigger, over and over, the dry click echoing over the sand and under the moon.

"Nothing will happen tonight," he said.

2

THINGS MY FATHER WILL
NEVER DO AGAIN

I entered the darkened barbershop in Istanbul, a wreck of a man with an unkempt beard. The barber, wearing a crisp blue work shirt, flipped a switch. Lights hummed, a singer crooned from a crackling radio, and a steel fan creaked to life. I had stopped caring months ago, and my face was a wall of curls.

What did I want? I had no idea. The barber nodded. With a sigh, I took a seat, and he wet my head with a spray bottle. I closed my eyes. Then my head began to spin. I was hung over, and the foul funk of grief burned in my throat.

Three months earlier, the doctors in Florida said my dad was very sick. On the X-ray I could see a ghostly starfish wrapped around his neck, suffocating pipes connecting head to heart.

The sound of scissors—click, click, click—took me back to the hospital. Opening my eyes, I watched as dark chunks of my hair fell to the ground. The barber paused to remove a straight razor from a paper sleeve, and I thought I smelled disinfectant. Into a bone handle went the blade, and I nearly retched.

The surgeons at the Mayo Clinic removed as much of my dad's tumor as possible, but it seemed too late—the stuff had probably spread to his bones and blood. He lay in the hospital bed, his neck a ruined gash, no longer able to eat or speak. As we prepared for an aggressive schedule of desperate radiation, we kept round-the-clock vigil, hours in a room echoing with medical beeps and alarms. Pleading with nurses—please administer the pain meds, but not too much, we want him to be able to walk; we need him alive enough to endure the radiation—we also stalked the physical therapy twins, two stout men who, if they would only come again, would see he was awake enough to stand, that he was well enough to live. Meanwhile, his stomach bloated on liquid food, and we took turns swabbing his blazing forehead with damp cloth. Then the pain came, and I watched as his eyes rolled into the back of his head. He screamed without sound.

My teeth chattered in the barber's chair, and I thought about the blood and meat in a man's neck and all that was required for that meat and blood to function. I looked up and saw the barber's knife hanging in the air, over my own neck.

At six foot two, my dad had been a legendary bon vivant, his graying pompadour a guide to the good life. He visited us in New York and we partied till dawn. He read all the right books. He wore six hundred dollar shoes he found on sale for thirty bucks. So it was a shock to see him, years later, arms limp, mute, delirious with pain, glasses crooked on his nose, gums atrophied from disuse. Dipping a towel into warm water, I rubbed shaving cream onto scratchy cheeks. It was a tense moment: He'd always been so particular about his toilet, and not only was I guaranteed not to shave him to his old standards, but, with all the blood thinners he'd taken, he also might bleed to death. There was no room for error. Those days, there was never room for error. Then, despite it all, a few weeks after the surgery, my dad was dead at fifty-nine.

The difficult part wasn't only that he was gone. No one likes it, but we're all prepared for this fact: Everyone, eventually, goes. The crueler agony for relatives of someone who'd died so quickly was that we, the living, having tried so hard in the hospital, having battled to keep him alive, after putting on all of our emotional armor, we were now supposed to take it all off again and go back to our regular lives. I tried. I'd just moved to Istanbul, allegedly one of the world's most fabulous cities. But hours and days seemed to slip away. And my wife was in Iraq.

The barber dragged the blade across my skin. He pushed my nose to one side, jabbing at stray hairs with flicks of his wrist. He held an earlobe in two strong fingers and drew a perfect line of hair down my chin. The singer's voice kept crackling on the radio, and a neat row of barber's brushes lined the wall. Sun streamed in through an open door. To my surprise—could it be true?—I found myself taking pleasure in something, in this case the barber's skill, this job done well.

Finished at last, the barber sat me up. I looked in the mirror. I was a son with a dead father, but also a young man with a new haircut. Laughing, I realized that I looked like Erik Estrada. Beaming at his handiwork, blow dryer roaring, the barber put away tools and rubbed lemon oil into my scalp. My hair had grown, now it was cut, and I bounded out into a new afternoon.

I wouldn't get another haircut for two years.

A CAUSE FOR CELEBRATION

From our balcony overlooking one of the cobblestone blocks not far from Istanbul's Taksim Square, I could reliably watch a dog or two scratching itself in the shade. Taxis and compact cars honked, parting a crowd of sun-drenched tourists gawking at shops selling instruments and trinkets or buying juice from the conservative guy downstairs. At night, a Joni Mitchell impersonator warbled for coins, keeping me up, and I wished upon her—and all the drunken revelers and the illegal construction workers choking the city night and day—a persistent laryngitis. All around us, meanwhile, a quiet war was going on.

It was summer, and I'd moved to Turkey a month earlier with my one-year-old daughter, Loretta, leaving behind the Saudi capital of deeply Islamic Riyadh, where my wife and I had lived for almost two years. I was relieved to have left: Saudi Arabia was an absolute monarchy, awash in new money, a third of its population guest workers, some of whom were treated like slaves. Booze was outlawed, and it was illegal for woman to drive or to appear uncovered in public. All our friends there ever seemed to do was eat, pray, or go to the mall.

All things considered, as hard as life was in Saudi, we managed to accomplish a lot—among other things, Kelly gave birth to our daughter and began filing more and more significant stories. Then her bosses offered her the posting in Baghdad.

Istanbul was supposed to be a kind of paradise. But several weeks into the new arrangement—Kelly in the middle of covering Baghdad for her first six-week rotation, me in Istanbul with our daughter, counting down the forty-five days until I'd see Kelly again—it felt like perhaps we'd made a huge mistake. Then my in-laws arrived for a three-week stay.

It's hard for me to describe just how hot Istanbul can feel in July. Perhaps the city is somehow closer to the sun or lacks a proper ozone layer. In any case, one evening, all of us panting in the heat, it was decided that my mother-in-law, Claudia, would babysit while I hit the town with my father-in-law, Steve. Claudia was a longtime eighth-grade history teacher in Lincoln, Illinois, a town of about fifteen thousand, where she taught in the same classroom for over forty years. While we went out, she was happy enough to stay home and read. Perhaps her visit to Saudi Arabia after Loretta was born had been enough of the Middle East for her.

Steve was a retired prison warden with enough of his old perimeter-securing instincts to consider an outing an adventure. Plus, there was a party. And Istanbul was one of the world's great cities. So with some gusto, he and I pounded down the warren of streets, past hundred-year-old buildings, many of them abandoned by the Greeks and Jews who'd been chased away. (Over two days in September 1955, riots in Turkey targeted Greek businesses and homes, the beginning of the end for a once-thriving minority population.) We walked down steep hills, trying not to get lost or be taken advantage of, our view enhanced by the occasional sight across the river of some of the loveliest mosques in all of Islam.

Rounding a bend, we finally came upon the incongruous but welcome sight of my American neighbor, Yigal's, book party. In the middle of the street, there stood a teeming mix of hundreds of stylish, smoking, and unshaven Turks and Westerners. I had no idea so many people would attend, and I felt both overwhelmed by the numbers and embarrassed by the distant impossibility of ever hosting my own book party. During seven years in the Middle East, Yigal had grown this luxurious beard, fathered two children, and co-written a beloved series of restaurant reviews, which was now a book. Since my dad died and Kelly had taken up a life in Iraq, all I seemed able to do was shave, worry, and buy milk.

The more I looked around, the more out of place I felt: the women—many in sheer, revealing dresses of various flimsy weights—all seemed to be drinking wine in stemmed glasses. The men—effortlessly rugged, bearded, wearing cool shoes—mostly held cans of Efes Pilsen, the local beer. I eyed my sandals and shorts, Steve clomping along behind me in white Reebok sneakers.

"I'll get us something to drink," I said.

We certainly weren't in Riyadh. The glass-fronted gallery had whitewashed walls and floors, giant metal bins filled with beer and ice. Lusciously framed images—pages blown up from the book—showed bean stews, grilled meat, and tomatoes throbbing with red ripeness. Everything felt fragile and impermanent, lovely and pleasurable. Then I saw my neighbor holding court and decided I'd buy a book. The thing was small but sturdy and printed on heavy stock and designed with a tasteful balance of text and illustration. Thinking of all the friends and relatives who would eventually visit us in Istanbul, I bought two.

Welcome to your new city, Yigal inscribed. *Eat your way to happiness.*

I popped a beer, thinking about happiness. Around me, the crowd seemed bigger than any Chelsea art opening I'd ever attended; it had a greater hum than an illegal Williamsburg loft party; but after all these years as an expat, could I be trusted to judge how cool—or doomed—any of it might be? I was already thinking ahead to how I would describe the scene to Kelly when I talked to her on my next scratchy call to Baghdad.

I found Steve and we perused the food carts set up in front of the gallery. There were long lines at the "cucumber man," a local purveyor who deftly cut the vegetable and dusted the elegant result with rock salt. There was also a baker whose glass cart displayed pastries stuffed with meat, cheese, or chocolate. The biggest crowd had gathered for a his-and-hers duo dishing out stews and fried vegetables. I waited for a wedge of fried zucchini to cool and overheard a young woman with blond hair say, in lightly accented English: "We *did not* go to Penn together. I met him later, in Boston."

Then the call to prayer rang out, a strange soundtrack for a massive party, and I looked up, noticing how tightly packed we were, hemmed in by old buildings, many of which had been resettled by Turks. There was nowhere for all the noise to go but up, and all the people above were hanging out the windows, staring at us: the shirtless man with a vast moustache, like some kind of retired Ottoman general, a cigarette between his thumb and forefinger; two grim women drinking tea and scowling on a balcony festooned with sunflowers; a gaggle of thin and dirty children opening and closing a second-floor window, cackling, throwing seeds.

Feeling uneasy, aware suddenly of how the world was both very big and very small, I squirmed at the rapid approach just then of a half-dozen men, each as grizzled as the next. They had paint splatters on their shoes and concrete dust in their hair. With none of the rolled-out-of-bed nonchalance of the hipsters surrounding us, these guys looked hungry, maybe angry. I watched them load plates and lean on a wall beside me. My pulse quickened when one saw me staring, but instead of hitting me, he made up a wrap from his heavily piled plate, stuffing a lettuce leaf with red paste, and then he handed it to me with such bonhomie I couldn't refuse.

I felt a hand on my shoulder.

"It's hot," Steve said. "I'm leaving."

I watched my father-in-law amble away, summiting the hill just before the arrival of a stout police wagon containing two swarthy officers in crisp shirts and peaked caps. This felt ominous. Indeed, the men were shock troops for Turkey's new ruling party and its neo-Islamic revival. For generations, the country's greatest icon was the military leader Ataturk with his legacy of strength and discipline that consecrated all things secular and orderly. Now the economy was booming. The various coups and military maneuvers of the past felt like distant relics. Religious fervor was now power's most important accessory. Yigal's partner stole over to the police wagon bearing platefuls of food. The men inside scowled and sniffed at the food, but they ate, and then they pulled away.

Maybe it would all work out? The book party, me without my wife, a city like Istanbul, which was balancing a burgeoning new art scene against a growing feeling among the masses, once again, that religion should dominate the public debate. I pushed back into the gallery and came across Yigal, who ran his hand through a mane of sweaty hair. The crowd was thinning rapidly.

Yigal looked crestfallen. "At least we've sold a bunch of books," he said. I asked him why he thought the party had been busted. Hadn't he done some advance work to make sure the neighbors were fine with a big party on their block? He told me the gallery was supposedly well liked—or at least tolerated. "We'll be okay," he said. It seemed like a question as much as an answer.

Then I spotted a war photographer I knew from Iraq. I stood off to the side, wondering if I should join. More police showed, and the photographer's entourage began to grow, everyone slouching and smoking—a mix of journalists, interns, admirers, filmmakers, graphic designers, writers—people from all over, the nomads who called Istanbul home, a brew of international whatever. People for whom everything was always okay, because they could always move on. Caring for Loretta, I could only move so fast or go so far, and then I'd be tugged back home.

The cops ordered us to leave. The TV reporter, blonde hair flying, emerged triumphantly from a store with a dozen bottles. Grabbing one, I was surprised by how easily I could smile, how instantly I could revert to a role I felt like I hadn't played since becoming a father. More police wagons rolled up and someone in our crew gave the cops the finger. We trudged away, visitors here, lights bouncing off walls, sirens fading. Someone threw a bottle, which exploded against the wall.

I found myself walking next to a Turkish woman who'd lived in New York. I told her everything. About Saudi, my in-laws, Kelly in Iraq, my daughter, my dad's horrible death, and how this was the first night I'd really gone out since moving here nearly a month ago. I told her I didn't really understand how to act like a person who enjoyed being out at night, throwing bottles against the wall, doing something like giving the cops the finger.

"Don't worry, just…enjoy. Oooo, look at him," she said, pointing at a tall, well-built man in our group. "I love this city."

Taxis crunched over the winding lane, headlights scissoring smoke. Bars were beginning to open and the night air was finally losing some of its dense heat. It felt like we had all the time in the world. At this point neither the Turkish lady nor I knew how much Istanbul was changing—that many of the bars would soon close, forced out of business when new decrees banned outdoor seating, part of a broad portfolio of heavy-handed and conservative legislation—that, indeed, the whole region was in flux. So much of the changes in Syria and Egypt and Iraq and beyond would feel bloody and final, but other moments would seem desperate and slightly insane. Just a few weeks later, not far from where we stood, young men would break up an art party by beating people with frozen oranges.

Our crowd hooted and hollered, smoked and laughed, as if nothing could go wrong. I told my new friend I wanted to get us more beer, and I ducked into a store, psyched about getting drunk and whatever else happened. I was up for anything. After two years in Saudi Arabia, the ability to buy liquor any time I wanted, and in any quantity and variety, was still a rush.

Inside, a cat sat on the register and an old man stared at me blankly. It took me a while to decide. I would later learn through trial and error that all beer in Turkey tasted the same, that the prices would continue to rise, that something fundamental was shifting. By the time I emerged with a heavy bag—after pondering how many bottles to get and counting out the proper change—I found, to my surprise, that everyone was already gone.

MY WIFE'S BODYGUARD

I watched as Ahmed Qusay Mustafa attempted to fit his giant body through the front door of our apartment in Istanbul. Head of Kelly's staff in Baghdad, Ahmed had a broad face, squinting eyes, and hands the size of toasters. For one night, during his layover before a flight to Washington, D.C., where he'd receive additional training, I'd be *his* caretaker—ironic because for two years he'd been taking care of Kelly.

First I showed him his room—my room, actually—and I was relieved when he touched the bed and found the softness to his liking. Alone in the kitchen, suddenly overwhelmed, I poured myself a glass of water, trying to remember how to say thank you in Arabic.

I finished my glass of water and tiptoed to Ahmed's room down the hallway. Baghdad felt very far away. It always did, but now, in Istanbul, I had a bit of Iraq in my bedroom. The door swung inside, revealing a man prone on the floor, smoothing out a bath towel.

"Which way?" he said.

I stood there, dumb. Then he raised his eyebrows, pointing first to the window, then to the wall, shrugging his shoulders. Understanding suddenly that the man wanted to pray, I pointed southeast, toward Mecca, in the direction of Saudi Arabia, a place I'd been trying to forget.

When he was done, we picked our way down busy streets. Ahmed wore a brand-new polo shirt, pressed slacks, and a pair of leather shoes. As a boy, he'd been to Germany with his father, but this was his first time out of the country as an adult. We walked to Akin Balik, an unassuming fish restaurant on the water where I'd spent many an afternoon alone. I tried to make him feel comfortable, pointing out a nice wooden table in the shade, a view of the boats. Out of instinct as much as anything else, I ordered us grilled sea bass, stuffed mussels, and a salad of arugula and olive oil.

It was a gorgeous afternoon under the kind of brilliant blue sky that makes a Turkish winter so majestic. But after a while, the sun felt a little too bright and I'd maybe ordered too many dishes and a street cat began its infernal whining. Ahmed picked at his food, taking photos of boats with a tiny camera. Absentmindedly, I motioned for a drink. When my can of beer arrived, Ahmed eyed me carefully.

"It's okay," he said. "No problem."

I was having a beer at lunch with a religious man.

After I paid the bill, we walked along the sea. Thin lines of fishing wire cut through the blue water, trash floating just below the surface. A row of restaurant touts shouted for business. One wore a wrinkled tuxedo, another too-tight jeans and a long-sleeve T-shirt, multiple Western logos sewn onto the sleeves.

"Bienvenue," he said, extending a menu.

"Arigato," said the guy in the tux.

"Shalom," said a guy with a Santa hat.

"Where are you from?" a final man called out. "Where are you going?"

Then we entered a four-hundred-year-old mosque—The New Mosque, actually—climbing worn stairs alongside a stream of worshippers and tourists. Stone walls reached for the sky, where a knot of white gulls pin wheeled in the air. The mosque was an amazing sight, the crown jewel, I suppose, of many a cluttered passport. I watched a wealthy European in starched pants stare in reverence at a line of ornate religious scripture. Ahmed looked bored.

"I don't need to see any more mosques," he said.

We took a ferry across the mighty Bosphorus. To break the silence, I suggested we order tea and sweets from the galley. Ahmed just shook his head. Meanwhile, a tanker sent blue water skidding across the channel, and I got to thinking: Back home in Iraq, oil was flowing, but what did that mean for a guy like Ahmed? I knew he'd socked away money to buy a shop. And he had a degree in engineering. But once the Americans were all gone, it was hard to say what lay ahead. The tanker receded in the distance, but there'd be another one behind it.

"We have a boat like this in my neighborhood," he said. "Before: Saddam's boat. Now: Our boat."

We climbed the old stairs to the apartment. In late evening twilight, I made tea and we chatted about our families. He'd brought a red teddy bear for Loretta. When you squeezed, the bear said, "I love you." Ahmed had a daughter not much older than ours. I regretted not having a gift for her. Then my phone beeped with a message from Kelly, writing from Baghdad.

Is everything all right? How is he?

How was she? That always felt like the more important question. Then Ahmed cleared his throat.

"I am turning thirty soon," he said.

I imagined a feast, perhaps on the old boat? Everyone who'd ever passed through Baghdad—myself and my wife and everyone else—could all converge. It could happen. It could be perfect.

"You totally deserve a big party," I said.

The big man shook his head. I watched him close his eyes, returning to a place I could only visit—a life I could scarcely imagine.

"Birthdays are for children," he said. "I am happy to be alive."

THE CANNIBAL BIRDS OF BURGAZADA

Our first glimpse of the island came as the sun dipped below the hills. I hefted luggage onto the dock. Kelly was in from Baghdad and we had planned a week's stay on Burgazada, one of seven islands a short ferry ride from Istanbul. The in-laws were there too, and I was excited. Family bonding was imminent.

Boats bobbed in blue waters, and a row of fish restaurants had tables with white tablecloths set out. We saw a patisserie with shelves of puddings and cakes. Next door was a grocery, a butcher, and a produce stand.

Up the slope was a seaside community, where locals summered in wooden houses and where we'd rented a large apartment. As we walked up the hill, flower boxes bulged with color and a wizened couple sat on a terrace sipping tea. A horse-drawn carriage rang its bell and we stepped aside.

Later on the wrap-around balcony, Kelly held tongs, beaming through smoke, and tended a roaring grill. Claudia and Steve oohed and aahed at the view of the pool. Candles flickered on a table, and the sun burned orange.

That night, I awoke to screeching. I turned to Kelly, hoping she was still asleep. With each piercing call, my brain hurt. It was hard to believe how loud it was, how many birds must have been out there, and why on earth were they making so much noise? I lay motionless in bed, trying to listen to Kelly's breathing, praying she was getting some rest. It was four AM.

At last, for an hour or two, we had quiet. But just before dawn, a rooster crowed and the gulls began screaming again. A dog barked, then another. Soon enough, our daughter Loretta woke up. I staggered into a blazing Turkish morning.

Groggily, I made coffee and rifled the cabinet for a box of UHT milk. Loretta padded around in bare feet. Then Kelly emerged from our room with wild hair and red eyes.

"What the fuck?" she said.

I looked through the window as a gull swooped low, screaming its terrible "caw." It shat in the pool, then sliced up and away, into the morning sky.

I went out to investigate.

Since I'd picked this place—visiting it during a cold and rainy afternoon earlier this spring—I felt a certain responsibility. Kelly had been in Iraq for a year, and this week was important. While it looked lovely from the terrace, up close the pool was a film of leaves, bugs, and feathers. The sky above was a riot of howling birds. I found a net and began to skim, dragging the surface, walking circles around the pool. In the grass, Loretta trundled around. "Toot, toot," she said, mimicking a ferry. Steve watched grimly from the balcony, slamming back a cup of coffee. Claudia took a long shower and Kelly came downstairs carrying the ropes and clips for a baby swing for Loretta.

I spotted a bone in the pool. Hoping Kelly hadn't seen—not wanting this vacation to become too macabre, desiring a break from such things—I scooped it up. Meat hung off the scalloped filigree of a spinal column and I tossed it into a bush. Feeling nauseated, I set again to skimming, working the net faster, hoping there'd be no more gore. On a nearby tree, Kelly set up the swing, and Loretta settled in for a push, laughing.

The birds continued to scream, and we tried to eat lunch. Sitting on the balcony, a view of a monastery in the distance, we peered into the sky. A gull and crow clashed in the sky, talons locked, retreating to rooftops to scream at each other. It was war.

The next morning, I again skimmed the pool, thinking, "Oh, this isn't so bad." Then a gull flew at my head, a whoosh of screaming. Attempting to avoid the bird's second pass, I nearly fell into the pool.

Then I saw the reason the gull was so upset. It was trying to protect its fledgling, a fluffy bird the size of a loaf of bread, which bleated plaintively and pecked at something in the grass. Then it lifted a foot into its feathers. It shat, skittering into the bushes. The tiny bird's mother circled overhead.

Walking closer, I inspected what the fledgling had been picking at. Bones and meat and blood—with the gristle torn off, a red smear on the concrete. In the pool, rolling in the current, two spines had already been pecked clean. The size and shape of the spines made it clear. The birds were eating each other.

After another mostly sleepless night, I stood on the balcony the following morning and eyed the water. Was it again filled with bugs and bones? Yes, it was. By a deck chair splattered in shit, the baby gull pecked at a meaty bone. I shuddered.

Around the kitchen, on the third day, morale was low. I made sure a pot of coffee was gurgling. None of us had slept the night through since we'd arrived.

"Fucking birds," I stammered, slicing into a peach.

"I hate them," my mother-in-law hissed.

Kelly and I went for a run, tracing the edge of the island to its western terminus. We'd been living apart for most of a year, but despite it all—and despite the cannibal birds—we had still managed to fall quickly back into a rhythm. The gulls thinned out in the hills, and we ran happily into hot wind, further away from the birds with every step. Her footfalls made time beside my own. Soon enough, Kelly would be back in Iraq.

We fell into a pattern: Coffee in the morning, a long breakfast. A run for Kelly and me. Claudia took the little girl on a long walk. Steve pushed her in the swing. We'd nap after lunch and swim through the afternoon. Feeling a sense of calm, I skimmed the pool enough to remove feathers and gore, climbed in, and looked up to see two birds locked in battle.

The days melted into one another, and to my immense relief, the bones and the cries of the birds eventually became part of the landscape, the background noise to our vacation routine.

On the second-to-last day, Loretta napped, and I stretched out in our bedroom. I heard Kelly in the lounge, Skyping with colleagues about flak jackets, battle helmets, and satellite phones. Sleepy and heartsick, I tiptoed out to give her a set of headphones, hoping to muffle half a conversation I didn't want to hear in the first place. I thought about how different my life was from my wife's. In

Istanbul, I was mainly a father, and each night I gave our daughter a bath, put her to bed, then cleaned up the house. Kelly, meanwhile, lived behind blast walls, guarded by men with machine guns. Why, when we came together, did there have to be cannibal birds?

For months afterward I would awake to images of creatures in the sky, tearing each other to bits. The birds' racket had infected my dreams.

But that last night on Burgazada, wrestling through the half-sleep of a fever dream, I saw a plane crash and a desperate search for survivors.

3

ANTHONY IS DEAD

It was one of the first warm evenings of Lebanon's spring when my new neighbor Steve—leaning over his balcony and through the bougainvillea—suggested that we should take the kids to Faraya, a ski town a few hours from what was starting to look like a war in Syria.

Kelly and I had just moved to Beirut, where we joined a crew of journalists and families, including legendary *New York Times* reporter Anthony Shadid, who'd encouraged my wife to come here in the first place. Beirut was, in theory, a plum assignment, with beaches, bars, and mountains like Faraya. After three years in the Middle East—the heat of Riyadh, the bombs of Baghdad, and the bleak solitude of Istanbul—we were all at last together. Loretta could walk and talk, Kelly had a new job, and I was ready for a fresh start.

"Sure, let's do it," I said, grateful for Steve's gesture of camaraderie.

Life was looking up.

* * *

The next morning, bright and early, Steve and I loaded up his SUV with bags of snacks and snowdrifts of warm clothing and a stack of CDs.

Beirut, when we drove through town that day, betrayed none of the horror we'd all eventually come to know. In the first months of 2012, downtown glittered with new buildings selling purses and Porsches, tourists and locals thronged new restaurants with fancy decor, and everywhere was more proof, it seemed, that we had made the right decision to come here.

Steve and I passed a Prada store and a Hermes shop and a few car dealerships and a TGI Fridays and a new mall and three Burger Kings and a Tony Roma's, and then, as we began the long, slow ascent, I saw vast tracts of shiny new apartment buildings, some with views of the sea.

Loretta sat happily in her car seat, munching a fig. Ed—Steve's blond son—had fallen asleep and was drooling prodigiously. On the stereo, a train named Thomas tried to understand why moving carts of coal was so important.

Soon we were surrounded by snow. Were you even allowed to park at a ski resort if you didn't ski? I didn't know. Any confidence in my ability to do anything right had been shattered years earlier, and I looked to a guy like Steve for direction. He had silver hair and a proud bearing. He prowled for a spot and the lot looked like a show room of luxury cars, dotted here and there by men and women prancing around in colorful, wintry snow gear. Lebanon was wealthy, and its colleges and natural wonders attracted Arabs from around the region. Though Steve and I were married to women with big jobs—his wife a dean at the business school and mine a newly minted bureau chief for NPR—the comfort and

spending power of many of the people around us exceeded anything we could ever scarcely hope to have ourselves.

Steve spotted an open space beside a gleaming BMW, but a
Mercedes beat us to it. He'd lived here for five years and knew
the game, gunning it toward a second spot right beside the slopes.
Then a security guard materialized. He carried a pistol on his hip
and gestured roughly for us to get the fuck out. We were not VIPs.
Just two dads in Beirut trying to go sledding.

"Daddy, I need to pee," Loretta said.

"Just wait a second, honey," I said.

Squirming in my seat, already shaking from cold, I reached for
my gloves, which were not there. I'd left them in the damn apartment. The little things could slip away from you. I felt my excitement about Beirut, about everything, beginning to fade.

Steve roared out of the lot, slicing through snow drifts, telling
me with a smile that he knew a second lot—and a bathroom—and
anyway, it'd probably be less crowded.

Sledding. With my new friend. What could go wrong?

At last, the four of us lumbered up the mountain through the cold.
Loretta wore three sweaters and a pair of Ed's snow pants. I wore
three scarfs and my late father's too-small wool hat. It had been a
long winter, and the snow was, to my eye at least, frozen solid. For
as far as I could see, the world was blanketed in a white hush.

"Right," Steve said, his cheeks going red. "Let's find a place to
build a snowman!"

We trudged past young men and women smoking cigarettes
and drinking wine, sitting in folding chairs or leaning beatifically on skis and poles and snowboards. Loretta's nose began
to run and even with the prescription sunglasses I wore I was

having trouble with depth perception. Stumbling, I rubbed my naked hands together, wondering: If I got frostbite, would I still be able to carry Loretta back to the car?

His lips chapping, eyes watering, Steve announced we'd arrived at the perfect spot. We all bent down to dig snow. The kids took turns pawing helplessly, like a pair of seals. Ed began to cry. Steve held him in his lap, rocking back and forth. I looked at Loretta, who stared up at the sky, eyes watering. She looked like her mom.

Wanting to do my part, I kicked at the hard-pack with the back of my heel, building up a pile of fluff. Steve saw what I was doing and followed suit. Loretta watched us, sneezed. Slowly, a quantity of malleable snow amassed. With the children eyeing us, Steve and I shaped three balls, my fingers going numb, and then we balanced one on top of another, making a little man not much bigger than a coffee can.

We regarded it in silence. As the sun angled better, I could see the vista was achingly beautiful, and I thought—as I had so many times—about what I would tell Kelly later.

Loretta pointed at the snowman's face, emphatic. She worked her jaws, looking for the right word.

"Eyes!" she said finally. "Daddy, he needs eyes! He can't see."

I couldn't argue and out of my pocket I withdrew two bottle caps. I screwed them into his face. "There," I said.

"Right," Steve said, shaking some snow off his pants and holding a squirming Ed in one arm. "Shall we sled?"

In Beirut, where everyone ran diesel generators between power outages, Steve often bemoaned the availability of fresh air. Now we had plenty of it, and I wondered if my face was as contorted by the cold as his.

I stood by an orange toboggan. It seemed small. I scanned the white expanse. Clouds swirled high above us. Skiers hurtled toward an inevitable conclusion at the bottom of the slopes. I sat upon a tiny orange disc and dug my heels in. Was that right? I was from Miami, and winter sports were a distant concept. Feeling it wanting to launch into orbit, to hurtle me down this hill my heart raced. The whole contraption was ready to go, so I grabbed for Loretta, who squealed, and as she worked her tiny muscles against mine, I crammed her into the space between my knees.

Plastic rocketed over snow, and we were hurtling downhill, scarves flying, wind whipping through hair, sun-blind and shivering. Loretta was dead silent, and as we hurtled down the white mountain, I wondered if this was another one of those moments when I'd dragged her into a situation she wasn't yet ready for. Wind whistled in my ears, and I regretted all the decisions I'd ever made, but then—halfway down the hill—she screamed with joy, and I discerned for a moment the difference between excitement and fear, between guilt and action—this, at last, was action we could both enjoy. The sled went faster and faster, no turning back, and then all of a sudden we were fishtailing, nearly flipping, and sweet Jesus, it could have been bad, but I took control. We glided to a stop, and I had not fucked it up.

The wind blew down off the mountain. I could hear the slicing sounds of skis cutting across snow and the happy murmur of people waiting in line for the ski lift.

"Again, Daddy?" a tiny voice said. "Can we do it again?"

A month later, spring had unleashed a season of squalls in Beirut. It wasn't as cold as Faraya, where we'd built the snowman, but every day rain seemed to slap against the pavement and storm drains overflowed, making everyone afraid to go outside. News from Syria was hard and heavy; days would go by without Kelly getting a full night's sleep. She'd work until midnight then wake up with her BlackBerry in her hand, only to begin typing again.

"Anthony is dead," I shouted, running down the hall into the bedroom. Kelly was still entombed in warm sheets.

She shot out of bed, ran to her computer, and a few minutes later was filing a news spot for NPR. Anthony had a son and a daughter and a wife and an ex-wife. Every weekend, Kelly had tried to plan a play date with him but news always got in the way. Now he was gone, and I'd never get to see him.

In a daze, I put Loretta into fresh clothes and watched Kelly pace the room. Rain came down in sheets. We were late for school, and I dreaded loading Loretta into the stroller. Kelly gave us a half-wave goodbye, her face pale and eyes red.

"Daddy, I'm cold," Loretta said, as I buckled her into the stroller. "It's bad out there."

Finally, in the shelter of my daughter's school, less than an hour since I'd heard the news, I held Loretta's hand, numb. Kelly, I worried, shouldn't be alone at this moment. I couldn't wait to get back, to talk about what this all meant for us—for everyone, for this new life we'd barely started living—but first I had to install Loretta into the embrace of one of her teachers.

In the middle of the hallway, surrounded by hand-painted posters and tiny backpacks, I was confused to find an administrator waiting for me. She smiled, clapping me on the back.

"Congratulations!" she said. "You should be so proud."

I was stunned.

It turned out, on that morning of all mornings, the school was announcing which of the children in the daycare program had been admitted into the kindergarten.

Back outside, under a steady rain, I stood shivering, holding an acceptance letter I didn't know what to do with. The water made the words bleed and the paper disintegrate.

On a brilliant Sunday a few weeks later, there was almost no chill in the air and a fat sun hung in the sky. Anthony was gone but we were still here. It was time for a family trip to the grocery store. Walking the sidewalk, I watched Loretta hold Kelly's hand, and in my own, I carried a bag of knives.

"That's poop!" Loretta squealed. "On the sidewalk!"

She laughed like this was the funniest thing she'd ever seen. Two more Western journalists had died in Syria since Anthony.

At the grocery store, Loretta demanded to ride in a shopping cart shaped like a car.

"It's dirty," Kelly said.

I looked inside. There was a steering wheel with a horn and a little seatbelt torn in half. There was also a dark puddle on the floorboard underneath the place a gas pedal should be. I sighed. We wanted to do everything right. Yet sometimes it was hard to know when to say no, to make the choice to walk away from what might harm us.

We walked past bins of produce, which we would wash in bottled water to avoid typhoid—which struck us all anyway later that spring. I paused at the cases of milk, trying to remember which of the four wasn't among the ones recalled because they were basically sugar-water dyed with chalk.

The girls scooted off to pick pasta and I walked to the meat counter, where I caught the attention of a younger guy with a wisp of a beard. I dragged a dull blade across the heel of my palm, trying to indicate the problem.

He nodded, understanding. I hated having dull knives. Puffing out his chest, the butcher settled a steel wand into a pink-stained butcher block. With great arcing swings of his arm, he slashed my blades over steel.

Mesmerized by the sound and sight and the smell of all the meat behind the counter, I couldn't stop thinking about Anthony and the other journalists who had been killed. At an informal gathering after his death, his assistant had come in wailing, repeating her departed boss's name over and over, beating her chest with grief. "Why did we let him go? Why did we do this?" Then I attended the funeral, where an entire generation of reporters sat in pews, heads bowed. It was tempting to think some of them might take a break—reassess or something. Unable to even fathom canceling a reporting trip, Kelly spent the hours of the funeral deep inside Yemen.

I watched the butcher slap down a giant hunk of imported Australian beef. It was probably one hundred dollars worth of meat, and my eyes grew wide. He showed me one of my knives, then he plunged the blade into the loin. Working feverishly, like a man possessed, he merrily sawed off a two-dollar chunk here, then a five-dollar hunk there, making a quick pile, which he proceeded to bludgeon until it was a pile of gore.

"Stop," I said. "I get it. They're sharp!"

The butcher took a deep breath, shook his head, as if to wake himself from some kind of dream, and then he began to whistle. Taking out a clean cloth, he wiped down each blade, laying them on the counter for me to inspect.

"These are good," he said. "Now they are better."

Walking home, I held my daughter's hand, and in the other hand I held a bag of knives. Kelly walked ahead of us, lost in thought. A few weeks later, fearing that the deterioration of security made a trip impossible, she'd cancel a trip into Syria. But she couldn't stay out forever.

WHEN I FINALLY SAW BLOOD

I'd lived in Beirut for nearly a year—next to the mess in Syria, where more than twenty thousand people had so far been killed. My wife routinely crossed the border trying to explain what was happening. I'd stay behind, caring for our young daughter, trying to make a go of it in our third city in the Middle East. The rains came and went, there was snow on the mountain and sporadic gunfire in the hills, and then—one clear night—we all gathered in the kitchen to make dinner.

Kelly had been posted in Baghdad for a year and a half. Those weren't fun times, spending so many months apart. Among other problems, it was difficult to be a man, changing diapers, while Kelly swash-buckled her way across Mesopotamia. With the mother of our daughter based in Baghdad, I learned how to excel at various domestic chores and also how to worry. What would happen if bad guys tested that one-hour bulletproof glass on her armored truck? What would people think of a blond woman traveling to Anbar Province? For Kelly, the Middle East was the big leagues. For me, it was a place to find a good doctor and maybe some daycare. Alone on a Friday night, I'd pour myself another glass and wonder: What could I do?

One thing I couldn't ever do in good taste was complain too much. After all, actual Iraqis had it much worse than I did, and their situation was only eclipsed by the growing number of Syrian refugees massed on the border, driven from their homes, living in the mud and the snow. Compared to any of them, I lived a princely life. But among my own people, I had trouble finding anyone to connect with. At least in the popular imagination, most journalist spouses were women—many of them back in America, almost all of them taking care of the kids. A whole generation of young Americans had flown to the same countries I had, but they were in the military, and their people were back on base or some military town they called home. I was in a strange city—confused, alone, and overwhelmed.

Being in beautiful but sometime unbearable Beirut was supposed to fix this. For one, Kelly and I would spend a lot more time together. Also, I was off round-the-clock diaper duty because our daughter was potty-trained and old enough for school. So we found an apartment in an old house, bought a bunch of furniture, and hired a carpenter to make shelves. We were almost ready to host our first dinner party when things began to unravel in Syria. The Syrian government was slaughtering its own people and peaceful protests had given way to an armed resistance.

Candles sat unlit on our dining room table, and Kelly worked eighteen-hour days. She obsessed over photos of a little boy with his head cut by army shrapnel and heard reports of other boys being tortured to death, their mutilated bodies delivered to their families. Then she learned about entire villages of people who'd been executed, throats slit. The worst was when a source would call, begging for help, and then his line would go dead. Kelly slept less and less, and the circles under her eyes deepened.

In December we learned a local friend and fellow expat was missing. His wife and baby were okay, but he was gone—killed by a fall during a recreational mountain climb. Friends gathered in mourning at their apartment, where I'd recently joined him and his family for Thanksgiving dinner. With dim recognition, I watched his wife stand there looking lost and holding their son.

A few weeks later, *New York Times* reporter Anthony Shadid had trouble breathing during a rugged crossing from Syria. He reportedly suffered an asthma attack and then perhaps a heart attack and then he was dead. At the memorial in a Beirut chapel, I sat in back and cried when I saw his son and wife. I left early to put our daughter to sleep. Kelly was out of town, far above sea level herself in the capital of Yemen, reporting on that country's slow lurch out of authoritarian rule. I hoped her own asthma wouldn't flare up.

Then it was a woman: Marie Colvin, *The Times* of London legend, who Kelly and I had met in a Beirut bar. Marie shook my hand and wished me the best. "Who do you work for?" she asked. "Myself," I said, and we clinked glasses. Kelly sort of looked like Marie, and I suppose they were alike in some ways, though Marie had no children. Her legacy was her career; in Sri Lanka, she'd lost an eye following the fighting, and in its place she wore a black patch.

Then Marie was gone, her body buried for a time in a shallow garden grave in Syria. She would always be remembered for her courage, admirers wrote. The photos of her death were ghastly, and I couldn't look. How could I? A blond woman dead in Syria? Kelly continued to cover the growing conflict. Her stories earned much praise. I worried, of course—I dreamt one night that Kelly was ordering a black eyepatch like Marie's—but I was also proud.

One night Kelly and I were hosting her company's security adviser, an ex British soldier. We sat on our balcony after dinner, drinking Lebanese wine, and then we started hearing pops, like fireworks. "Must be someone celebrating," I joked. Then we heard many more pops, and it became clear these weren't fireworks. "Hah, hah," I said, "it must be happy shots, like after an important soccer match." But the firing grew more insistent, then constant, then deafening, and we retreated inside. Through our windows we saw soldiers pulling up in armored personnel carriers. They took firing positions on our front steps. I found that my right eye would not stop twitching. Then I slipped into our bedroom where I intended to drink until I felt calm or at least fell asleep. Kelly and her adviser, meanwhile, rushed out the door. Over the next seven hours, I slipped in and out of a stupor, taking care to see that our daughter remained asleep. I was relieved when Kelly finally came home.

Early the next morning, exhausted but also kind of thrilled, we watched the troops pull away, the skirmish revealed for what it was—a loud but contained criminal affair—and then our little girl was awake, running around in her pajamas. "That's a really big truck!" she said, pointing at an APC.

It should've been jarring to have the military on our block. It wasn't. Even with its arrival—literally at our doorstep—a little bit of violence hadn't altered our essential calculus, which had been ratified by the Kelly's security adviser, and by implication, the company: We were here, this was our life, and the risks were worth it.

The weather warmed, summer came and went, and the flowers on our balcony bloomed. It was late August, with temperatures and tempers mellowing, and our daughter was excited for her first day of school. We went to the beach, signed the girl up for swimming lessons, and sketched out plans for a long-delayed party.

Dinner that night was minestrone with pesto, which was lovely, and one of my favorites. But it needed cheese. I eyed a block of Parmesan and grabbed our biggest knife. Shifting my weight, intent on a clean cut, I was momentarily distracted. The blade slipped and sliced through my thumb—a shock, how easily it fell through fingernail and skin—and the path was so clean—it went nearly all the way through—that for a moment I was actually, even as the blood began flowing, proud that I bothered keeping our knives so sharp.

I held up the thumb, blood streaming down my arm, shocked by the reality of the pain. This is how it feels! It was funny: All that worrying about Kelly in danger, and I, the guy who mostly worked at home or in a café, was the first of us to bleed.

Yet I couldn't help it, and I began to howl. It was a low, animal wail—a welling up of anger and sadness. Anger about a world that made me worry for our safety in the first place. Sadness because I could never worry enough.

So my thumb bled, and my daughter grabbed my leg. Kelly dropped the soup ladle, and I ran to our bathroom for a bandage and ointment. I stared at myself in the mirror, maybe a little embarrassed. Kelly was readying for another clandestine border crossing, and all I'd gotten was a kitchen cut. I looked at a reflection of a man holding his arm in the air, hand wrapped in a bloody towel. Then I walked into the kitchen, grabbed a bowl of soup, and among the charms and terrors of our life in Beirut, I took my seat at the table.

PEOPLE LIKE US

Kelly and I were entertaining an old friend, the new bureau chief for a major news organization, on our leafy terrace in Beirut. She had just moved to town and was scouting out houses before she brought over her husband and young children. I recounted how just a few weeks earlier, a massive, seven-hour shootout raged just below our balcony. How I had cowered in our bedroom beside a sleeping Loretta as thousands of rounds of machine gun fire went off. How Lebanese soldiers arrived in camouflaged armored personnel carriers, and how seven or eight grenades exploded. How I had feared for our lives and how, during some of the worst of it, instead of cowering beside me, my wife Kelly had put down her wine glass, grabbed a notebook, and walked off into the night.

I didn't imagine I'd actually frighten our guest, herself a correspondent, who, like Kelly, was expected to make the insane counterintuitive step and move toward rather than away from gunfire. But as I described the night—how every loud noise since then had made me wonder if the battle had begun again, how I had refined my already elaborate plans for hiding and escape—my eye would not stop twitching, and I saw in this powerful woman something I recognized. It wasn't the blank stares or the sympathetic nod of misunderstanding or the bewildered sigh I usually got from friends here. They didn't seem capable of worrying. Was it the tightening of her grip on the chair, her sweaty brow, the mental checklist she herself seemed to be making as I talked? In this woman, I realized, perhaps I had found someone like myself.

"For people like us," she said, "Beirut is perfect. The constant soundtrack of worry inside ours heads is finally and totally justified."

We looked out over a black city twinkling with lights, at a thousand possibilities. Taking my glass to my lips, I sipped, nodded, sipped. The woman leaned back in her chair, smiling at me, eyes on fire.

Another morning my mom issued a Facebook post that alluded to a problem with a recent mammogram. *Send prayers*, the post read.

I tried to remain calm, but as I cleaned up the kitchen after breakfast, I found myself slamming the coffee maker into the sink, banging my head against the cabinets, sighing with frustration. Not only was I filled with worry, I was furious.

Kelly admitted she had seen the post the night before—it had been our ninth wedding anniversary—and not wanting to ruin the evening celebration, for which we'd planned a meal at a new restaurant in Beirut's Mar Mikhael neighborhood, she'd done what I wasn't able to do: she had pushed the bad news out of her mind.

I'd made it through the birth of our daughter in Saudi Arabia. Then my dad died abruptly of cancer, out of his mind with grueling pain. Then my wife began to work in various battle zones, and I'd had to learn how to be a single parent for weeks at a time—to hold

Loretta down as she writhed with a high fever, conversing with a doctor who spoke only Turkish as he jabbed her in the stomach with a needle. Over the years I had become quite accustomed to treating bad news and adversity as a calling, as opportunities to find uncommon utility and beauty in the simple act of fearing what might happen next.

For twelve hours I'd been in the dark about the state of my mom's breast. This was agony for a guy who'd practically become a bad-news addict. I'd lost out on hours of preparation. And with the time difference, it'd be another several hours before she woke up. I retreated to the bedroom, closed the shutters, pulled up the covers, and ruminated.

All over again, I had this urgent yearning to act. I did the math for how long it would take to get to America, where I would stay, and which hospital was closest, and then I thought in vivid detail about the beeps and the squeaks and the smells and the tastes and all the life-and-death drama of doing battle in another hospital room. I thought about my mom's house and her pets and her insurance and her will, and had she said something about being cremated? Did she have a special song she wanted us to play at the funeral? Sweat ran down my face and a car backfired—or maybe it was shots?—and finally my mom wrote saying that she was up. She'd call soon and we could talk.

It isn't always pleasant for Kelly, all this worrying. She has suggested we might be happier if I let go, if I "rolled with the flow." But the flow, at least as she construes it, can be insane—involving as it does the whole battle helmet/flak jacket thing—and yet somehow she happily rolls with it.

We are different, Kelly and I. In the back of a taxi, for example, after her return from somewhere deadly, she'll blithely daydream, planning the next trip to Syria or wherever, and I, meanwhile, will worry about whether or not the taxi driver will kidnap us. Or overcharge us. Or perhaps, if I am not vigilant enough, he might take a wrong turn causing us to be late.

I suppose I take some crazy pride in all this overthinking. This hand-clenching fear in the back of a taxi. In a way, I suppose I could even point, in theory, to all that this worrying makes possible, such as my punctuality. And, also what it prevents, such as us being kidnapped. But in reality, I admit, most of the time, the fact that I think too much probably leads more often to an increase in my personal misery—in a ratio disproportionate to the timeliness it occasions or the abductions it prevents.

The phone rang and I dashed into the living room, fretting at what I was about to learn yet eager to begin to plan, to think of every possible attack to keep my mom alive. Instead, her cheery voice asked about our anniversary, what we did, what did we drink, and oh, was it fun? And for a moment I was flooded with happiness and relief, reflecting on the nice night Kelly and I had, how we had been married for nine years, moving houses from one strange foreign capital to another, how in Beirut we were able to have a lovely dinner at a cool new restaurant, where a good Manhattan whiskey cocktail was on offer.

"Yeah, so for the Manhattan they used Jim Beam, which was fine, because, really, that's a perfectly fine bourbon," I said. And then I recounted the bartender's deft use of an orange wedge. As I ran out of nice things to say about the anniversary, I began to regress into a sort of hyper-worry. And all along it hadn't yet occurred to me, because there was a mix of self-involvement and arrogance in my worrying. Let's admit it: My mom probably missed her husband and was no doubt capable of worrying all by herself.

"And, yeah, they used just the right amount of bitters, and… Mom, tell me about the goddamned scan."

I could hear her breathing.

Mammogram. What a word. So innocuous and mellifluous, like some sort of nursery rhyme, or mnemonic. I loved her and had loved my dad, and from his cruel situation I had demanded the unreasonable. I had thought that if a son wanted it bad enough, that if we all only tried hard enough, my dad could live forever—or at least longer than tomorrow or the next day. All around us, in the Middle East, friends were dying, people I'd never met were dying, and I had every reason in the world not to feel sorry for myself, but I did, and I just couldn't deal with my mom being sick.

"I think all they saw were the ghosts of an old scar," she said. "It's probably nothing. We'll know more Monday, okay?"

Kelly and I were invited to a party that night in a lovely backyard garden. Everyone wore linen or chambray or whatever, and I tried not to think about ghosts or what it meant to say, "It's probably nothing." What it meant to roll with the flow. Our friend and colleague—my fellow worrier—was there, and she and I gave each other meaningful nods.

I drank too much wine, and on the way back home, arm in arm, bubbly and happy, Kelly and I took turns pushing our daughter's stroller down a city sidewalk, and though she was just three years old, healthy and pink, and we were still somewhat young ourselves, blessed and apparently hitting our stride, it nonetheless seemed, to me at least, that despite all the evidence to the contrary, the path before us stretched on and on into an endless darkness.

BEND, DON'T BREAK

One day in Beirut I found myself inexplicably entering a room with mirrored walls. The space was hushed, with soft light from recessed bulbs. Hesitating, I tiptoed to a spot by the wall, unsure—unsure of what? Of everything, really. Then I laid out my watch, put my phone on silent, and took a deep breath.

On green mats all around me, creatures writhed in tight clothing. I stood still and tried to look as if I belonged here, to breathe as if I thought this might work. Inside, I was thinking we were all doomed, that our hearts were impure and we cared about the wrong things, and it couldn't be helped and nothing could be done. My heart was beating too hard and I was sweating already. Nothing good could come from this. Do you stand on the mat? Or sit on it?

It wasn't totally inexplicable why I had come here. I needed to chill, to roll with the flow, as my wife said. So I thought maybe the answer was yoga. It sounded so...ethereal. And these didn't feel like ethereal times here in Beirut. They didn't feel like ethereal times anywhere, really. An ugly election was playing out back home in the United States, a war was creeping over the border with Syria, and there was a general absence of anything to feel proud of or comfortable with or confident about. Yet yoga could set you free. I heard that no matter where you were, if you tried hard enough, yoga could make you buff and calm and happy and untroubled. These were things I wanted. Things I maybe deserved.

I sought a friendly face, but the women—it was all women—seemed shut off to the world. Each was in the middle of doing some bendy bendy. There was a slow flurry of limbs, all these special poses, each of which seemed to say: I am at rest, I am lithe, and the world is ready to let me do this. I wasn't so sure the world was ready to let me do this. More to the point, I was surrounded by nearly naked ladies, some of them Lebanese, some of them Western, none of whom ever met my eyes. We spoke no words. The woman beside me bent over, a strange salute from her hindquarters, almost like, *Hey, friend, is this so hard? Why the sad face? Be here with us, doing this, now.*

In walked the instructor, Tania, who might have been Lebanese or possibly Syrian. It was hard to tell. She had olive skin and severe eyebrows and seemed nearly seven feet tall. An impressive layering of scarves and sweaters hung about her, as if she'd just descended from some inclement mountain. I sat down and hugged my knees, fearful and grateful at once. It might hurt, but at least there was someone to tell me what to do.

Tania took a spot on a special mat and sat in the lotus position. The room filled with the warm sounds of world music, underscored with the sharp rat-ta-tat of gunfire, it seemed to me. I was hearing things. My heart ran like a baby gazelle in my broad, manly chest. But I am lying. I do not have a broad, manly chest.

"You," she said, extending a long finger. "You have not done this before."

I hung my head.

"Just breathe," she said.

Only then did I realize I hadn't been.

Soon enough, my body stretched into an allegedly restful pose. Tania said it was restful. She said it was called "downward dog." Then I lifted a leg into the air, holding it well beyond the point any-one would want to hold a leg in the air. It hurt. I desired to put my leg down. But I did not. Because Tania had not told me that I could yet. At her command I lowered that leg and lifted the other. Soon I was lifting a leg and an arm.

All of a sudden, in a different pose, I had my legs up over my head, supporting myself with bent arms, doing a shoulder stand.

"You must be careful," said Tania, running over. She eased me back to the ground. "You're not ready for this yet."

I thought about how easily people could get hurt. Syria was a war zone. In my daily life, I consorted with a handful of the people, including Kelly, tasked with making sense of what was going on without dying. And yet someone among us had to remember to buy milk. Then there was also drinking: we had all become quite good at that.

With Tania's instruction I felt previously unknown muscles twitch in my thighs, abdomen, biceps, calves, lower back. My toes and even my arches seemed to buzz. It was harder than anything I'd ever done before. Yet there wasn't much risk of failure. So often self-improvement was self-directed, a walk down a strange path. How comforting, in a world of unknowns, to have signed up for a guided tour.

For the last ten minutes we lay in silence. Tania crept beside me, hands again on my arm, showing me how to relax, and then she pulled down the collar of my shirt and rubbed some kind of scented oil into my neck and ears.

Over weeks and months, I grew stronger. The pain in my muscles gave way to tightness, an ability to balance, a steady breath. Oh, sure, I could still sense darkness gnawing at the edges. Nevertheless, every day, for nearly two hours, I could enter a room where everything was right, a small place bathed in light. I'd put my faith in Tania. And so, for at least some of the day, there were no gnawing questions, just a series of softly spoken answers.

Then, one day, before class began, Tania announced that she was leaving. "Class, this is my last session," she said. "I'm sorry to leave you." She hung her head. She instructed us all to close our eyes. I opened mine and saw that even Tania's were closed.

A few days later, unfamiliar Greta sat in Tania's spot. Her movements were hurried and preening, and she tossed her gorgeous hair a lot. Her music was loud. She seemed interested in her own body and its smooth moves, but not so much in how her students were doing. Covered in sweat, I walked out. I would never return.

Throughout Tania's final class I had wanted to scream, "Straighten your back, Tania! Strong spine!"

And afterward, putting away our mats, I heard whispers about a daughter in trouble, a flight to America, a new job. It had never occurred to me that Tania might have a life of her own, her own questions, her own darkness.

4

HOMELAND IN MY HOMELAND

Because I called Beirut home, and because an Amer-
ican TV show called *Homeland* won a bunch of awards depicting
my home, and because this depiction focused on Hamra Street—
which I crossed a dozen times a day en route to my butcher,
baker, gym, my child's school, and the café where I write—and
because this depiction was ham-handed enough to have enraged
the minister of tourism, who was spending millions attempting to lure tourists back to a beautiful and tragic city, and on top
of all that, because the show was originally an Israeli TV pilot,
an agonizing fact for a country still technically at war with that
Israel, and as if that weren't bad enough because the purport-
ed Beirut scenery was reportedly shot on location in the Israeli
towns of Tel Aviv and Haifa, I decided one Friday to describe a
typical day on Hamra Street, which turned out to be much more
like an episode of *Homeland* than I ever could have imagined.

*   *   *

I normally walk my three-year-old to school, but this Friday she wakes with a fever for the third day in a row, so instead I take her to the doctor. I call Hussein, who arrives in a lightly armored Mercedes. Loretta's pissed she's not going to class, so she squirms and kicks my seat. I beg her to sit still and look out the window.

We pass the Saudi embassy, where two hundred people stand baking in the sun, waiting for their visas, which they need in order to complete Hajj, the annual pilgrimage that all Muslims are compelled to complete at least once. To prevent corruption, the Saudis annually give each country a number of Hajj visas proportional to each nation's Muslim population. So pretty much anyone standing in line on a sizzling October in Friday has won a spot in the lottery. Spots are offered randomly and with shockingly little corruption, so the people in line are a motley and diverse mix— not my neighborhood's typical crowd of college kids, sad old men, and rich businessmen with their trophy wives. There's hardcore Bedouin guys in dirty robes and checkered headdresses alongside wide packs of women wearing abayas. The line pulses against metal barriers and soldiers with guns stand beside an armored personnel carrier nearby a series of giant asterisk-shaped iron ties installed in the road to prevent anyone from parking close enough to detonate a booby-trapped car.

We arrive at the hospital, which is affiliated with Johns Hopkins. The doctor frowns, telling me Loretta's been sick so long we need blood work and a urine culture. At the lab, I hold my daughter in my arms and she shudders. "Daddy, it hurts," she says, and I apply pressure to the needle's entry point.

Back at home, the babysitter arrives. Loretta naps, and I throw on a light cotton shirt for the walk downtown, where I'll meet a friend for lunch. The path takes me the entire length of Hamra. I pass the shuttered Applebee's, which will reopen elsewhere; my liquor store, which lately stocks Maker's Mark; the post office, where I'm sad not to discover the book I need to review but happy enough to find the last two issues of *The New Yorker*; and the local headquarters of the Syrian Socialist National Party, which is aligned with the Syrian regime.

In an alley I spot a guy with a series of snakes and barbed wire tattooed to his arms and neck. He's making coffee on a machine set into the back of a busted-up minivan on blocks. He glares at me, and I see in his eyes a guy who would happily beat me to death. Posters of what I assume are martyrs have been pasted to surrounding walls, and the swastika-looking flag of the SSNP is sagging from poles bolted to the walls of surrounding buildings.

Downtown—which had been rubble until five years ago, when it was recast as a luxury mall—Mike and I share a lunch of Lebanese salads and a tureen of hummus. Mike's wife will give birth to their son at the end of the month, and they've tried to meet every member of the hospital staff, imploring them not give her any drugs during the delivery. Reviewing the plan, Mike's wife asked him: "Are you sure you can watch me writhe in pain?" Mike admits he's not sure. I told him about how our daughter had been born in Riyadh and that we'd fought to have a natural birth.

We talk about all the people we know who died last winter and spring—Marie and Anthony and a French photographer named Remi and our mutual friend John, amongst others. I tell Mike I thought about not coming back this summer, staying in America forever, and I take a bite of hummus and bemoan how dark and unnatural it is to live voluntarily beside the miasma of death and destruction that is Syria.

I realize that for those who watch *Homeland*, Beirut must seem as dark as it does to us, equally as unnatural. And some of that is rooted in reality, in the persistent echo of years-old news stories.

In a taxi on the way back to Hamra, I pass the site of the massive car bomb that killed the Prime Minister in 2005. The driver takes a shortcut and I see the Hilton hotel tower, owned by Kuwaiti royalty, ruined in skirmishes during Lebanon's fifteen-year Civil War, trees growing from suites on the upper floors. But on first glance the view along most of the streets around here looks a lot like Queens.

Likewise, on first glance, you might conclude *Homeland* is a reasonably nuanced portrait of the war on terror, whatever that is. A portrait, anyway. The second season brought the action to Beirut, where CIA agents were made to grapple with a neighborhood that was hilariously (to people who lived here) crawling with snipers and warlords. The scene that allegedly depicted Hamra Street— where you'll find two busy lanes of traffic at all times cutting through a series of thriving restaurants and night clubs, a Crowne Plaza and a new H&M—showed a narrow alley lined with sandbags and desert people, everyone waiting to be shot at.

On those same blocks, in real life, on the day I want to show you all how nice Beirut is, I stop at Café Younes, in the center of the Hamra, where most afternoons I crack open my laptop for a few hours and nurse a French press. The syrupy voice of Lebanese singer Fairuz bleeds from the café's speakers, and every table is packed with students and reporters and silver-haired amateur philosophers and Syrian activists and grizzled NGO workers. Next door is an art gallery. Hanging from a pole in front is an arty jumble of rebar, bits of concrete sticking to the metal, the whole thing lit up by fairy lights. A fan above spins lazily. At three PM the power goes out and no one notices. You can literally set your watch by the outages here.

It's easy to assume *Homeland* didn't bother to send any scouts to Beirut. The tickets are expensive. It's just as easy to poke fun at their solution—send a bunch of actors to Israel. But don't we accept this of fiction? Haven't we always? You make choices, you build a space, you choose your details—and whatever you build, whether on the page or on the screen, it's never complete. "That's not Beirut," you say. What makes *Homeland*'s portrayal downright silly is the incongruity between the Beirut in the show and the Beirut in which I'm raising our daughter.

As if on cue, reality and fiction converge. The power flickers on, and my Twitter feed loads: A car bomb has just exploded across town. My phone won't dial out. I spill hot coffee on my foot. I feel punched in the face. The explosion wasn't far from where I had lunch, and I flash to Mike, his wife, their unborn child. I watch a girl sip a strawberry smoothie, a boy bite into a sandwich, and an old man struggle to plug in a new iPhone. A sexy lady is smoking Gitanes by the window, and her boyfriend lights a Marlboro. I scramble across the news updates on an Internet that barely functions trying to figure out what's going on, and the café owner's daughter leans on a car outside, smoothing her curly hair.

Emails start flying around. Can you get to the street by car? Phones not working. A photo. Looks small. No injuries? Then another photo. Lots of damage. One dead. Use BlackBerry messenger to get through. It's two dead. Two. Only two? A dozen wounded. Security sources are confirming. No, definitely many more dead. More than one hundred wounded? A giant crater?

In the rush of information, time slows down, and I take in the event as if watching a drama on TV—but this action is taking place just three miles from where I sit peacefully in my favorite café. The waiter brings more coffee. A scooter squirts by, roaring up Hamra, making its little burping noises. A man and woman embrace on a couch. That girl I've seen around, probably a freshman at the local design school, is wearing a blue feather in her hair and there are pink caps on the tips of her little leather oxfords. She's upset about something. She takes a seat and scribbles in a notebook, holding back tears.

I make the mistake of looking at some grizzly photos from the bombsite. I still have not heard from Mike. Cars are mangled and several firefighters stand in the smoking wreck that was once someone's apartment. The death toll is now eight in some reports, three in others. In one shot a woman covered in blood is fainting— in another photo I see what looks like the brains of a ten-year-old girl. An alert pops up on my phone, a reminder that Loretta's swim lesson is tomorrow at 4:30 PM.

If my life were a TV show, this might be the moment I have some kind of epiphany. Instead, heading home from the café, I stop for wine and a handle of whiskey and I pass a young boy with dirty fingernails flipping through a gun catalog. Tofu is back in stock at the health store and the phones work again; Mike calls.

"I just wanted to let you know we're okay," he says.

There's an American tourist in Wrangler jeans looking up, guidebook in her hand, and I get a good look at her long white throat. A man in front of his clothing boutique argues about the cut of a shelf in his remodeled front window.

Back at home, trying to remain calm, Kelly and I invite our friend Richard and his daughter to come by. His wife is on assignment in Libya and none of us want to be alone. I offer to stir up a round of Manhattans. Richard, who is from Wales, says he's never had one. I mix and we stare at our phones, seeking more information about our lives, and as it comes, our little girls run around, cutting things with scissors. It turns out one of the country's top intelligence chiefs is among the dead. We brace ourselves for the additional ugliness that is sure to come, and into each drink, I carefully spoon a bright red cherry.

I hand Richard his Manhattan, and he says he feels like a character in *Mad Men*. I feel the sting of the Hollywood comparison. He takes a sip, and I wait for his reaction.

"You Americans like everything so sweet," he says with a slight smile.

Later, I walk outside, toward Hamra Street, an American in Beirut heading to an ATM for some extra money, just to be on the safe side. My life is not a TV show. The streets are eerily quiet. If someone in Hollywood had written this, my character would do something brave. Or something stupid. Or maybe he'd be killed. In the faint light of a street lamp. A family of three is walking toward me and they're all licking ice cream cones.

FRIDAY WAS THE BOMB

I walk down the block to the nearest ATM as the lights in Lebanon flicker. I think to book tickets to anywhere but here. But the websites won't work and the travel agent is closed. Everything is closed. The streets are empty. Security gates are locked. I return to the house. Our friend Richard is gone, having consumed the too-sweet cocktail I made him. Kelly is on the phone with an editor. The already shitty Internet slows to a crawl. I check the fridge. There's almost no milk, and our daughter—cherubic three-year-old Loretta—might wake up any minute and cry, though she almost never does that. Not in Riyadh, not in Istanbul, not even that crazy night in Beirut the previous spring when there was a seven-hour gunfight on our block. Even then, with men in full combat gear on our front steps, their APCs parked in the alley, bullet casings bouncing off the concrete, she slept, and still we didn't leave. Tonight is somehow different. A very big bomb has exploded not far away killing the country's intelligence chief. Many will applaud his death. Others will seek revenge. This is the way things work here. Like in 1983, when the U.S. Marine barracks were bombed, this could be the beginning of the end. It's 2012, nearly thirty years later. The Syrian uprising is now a civil war, and all across the city ten thousand families are reconsidering their plans.

And what had been a low boil of panic becomes an all-out grease fire. I have been managing as best as I can, but it is increasingly difficult to be super excited about Kelly's job as a Middle East reporter as she repeatedly sneaks across the border into Syria, rushing toward the bang-bang, getting the story from the bad guys at every turn. No matter how important the news or however many precautions Kelly might take, the math is grim, the consequences inescapable. Colleagues have been killed, and it feels like it's just a matter of time.

Our life here is quite good most of the time. Our daughter does indeed go to an excellent school—the best, really—and we have so many friends, and I have begun writing again, and the beach is warm and the mountains cool. But there is a creeping sense that some final kind of darkness will soon be upon us. I remember exactly where I sat at the last funeral. I know where I've stashed the program, and I remember who gave speeches. I don't want to return to that chapel.

I stand on our plant-choked balcony an hour or two from Damascus thinking about what has come and what is coming, and maybe the booze is doing its trick or maybe it's adrenaline, but the little lava handshake occurring in my mouth is maybe helping me feel a little more brave or at least a little more detached from my body and the people I love. It's like I could float away, high above the city, see it finally for its great and rightly size. But then my mind brings me back to the block of rubble and the one hundred wounded, to the three dead, to the image of a father rushing past mangled cars with a bleeding girl in his arms. Is this man already at the airport with what's left of his family?

Then I am thinking: Maybe I should go lighter on the vermouth next time? Should I make more ice? I stare into our freezer, the cool darkness and the quiet, the orderly rows of whatever, and I become convinced that yes, we have plenty of ice. Enough to last all night.

Friday was the bomb, and it is now Saturday morning. The ice in my drink has melted and we parents are gathering at the park, where we are more hungover than usual. (There's always this plan to bring a pitcher of margaritas, or at least a thermos of coffee, but instead we're always clutching animal crackers and tiny sun hats.) We sit in the shade and watch our children run around, their small faces reddening, their skin slick with lotion. The really intense mom—an exasperated lady who is probably a better parent than all of us and who is always super patient with her two kids and always speaking Arabic and acting cool—she says she'll never leave, that her husband is Lebanese and she's raising her kids to be locals. And yet she always makes sure to have a supply of Cheerios. Her Arab children eat almost exclusively these American Os, which are really very tasty. Meanwhile, an olive-skinned American husband and wife are going straight to a conference in Denver, where they will drink good beer and contemplate staying for good. There is no direct flight from Lebanon to the U.S.

Richard is married to a French woman, who is like a preoccupied film starlet somewhere in her fifth decade, and she travels almost as much as Kelly and because of that feels as much at home in Libya as in a smart leather trench coat here in Beirut. Today Richard is alone, his eyes working madly, us dads always a bit of a mess when our women are gone, and I notice sweat running down his forehead. I have to admit I am always sweating, my wife in Iraq or Yemen or somewhere worse, while I spend so much time accounting for things—and then I realize my Welsh friend with the adorable accent can't find his three-year-old-daughter, same age as mine, and this is why he is particularly agitated. So he and I, imbued with clarity of purpose—which I'm momentarily awed to find I'm still capable of—dash around the soft padding of the playground, searching, looking behind slides and among screaming children for a little girl.

A parade of tanks drives by going faster than I would expect, treads clanking on the asphalt—a sound you never want to hear— but, now that I think about it, the tanks may have gone by the following weekend, when we were back at the park again. It is now much later, and I am having trouble remembering...

We think we have lost one of the children and it is a horrible feeling and I try to keep my eyes on my own girl, and then at last there is Charlotte, and we smile and laugh, and we sit down to hummus and bread and there's this shared sense that we are all a group of people in something together and we will remain this way for at least the duration of the morning here in the park. In this kind of community someone is always going home, alive or dead, leaving the others behind.

We walk home from the park and I hold my girl's hand and my wife smiles in the sun and a big BMW nearly runs us over. I see, in the window, the ghoulish smile of a man who doesn't give a fuck and I wonder, what is it like not to care? In front of the police station there's a son and his middle-aged mother. I try to imagine what they were doing during the various minor clashes that erupted last night after the bombing, when people set dumpsters on fire and fired shots into the air and shook their assault rifles at each other, when the tear in the fabric ripped a little more. Did this guy fire off some rounds? Did his mother call for someone's blood? Looking at them, I cannot at this moment picture the mother calling for blood or the son shooting me in the stomach. Indeed, they have that annoyed look of suburban people who are seeking police assistance maybe because someone said harsh words to their pet or upturned a planter at their house or some other minor annoyance that was not good but also not that bad. Sigh.

I'm not asking for much, just to have things blow up less frequently. Or not at all. Or at least when they blow, maybe no one could be ripped to pieces?

That's the thing: Dogs get walked or lost, the playground is safe or it's not. I can hear the cats crying in the bushes or maybe it's someone in pain, and you never know exactly how the mounting violence, or at least the threat of violence, is going to make you feel, how it's going to affect your wife, your friends at the park, or your daughter's ability or willingness to hold your hand. For now she is young enough that she will endure whatever I've asked her to endure and she will not run away and I will not let her disappear or be flattened by the tires of a giant BMW.

Then it's Monday, and I'm relieved to see the milk truck making its delivery. I am having trouble recalling Sunday because, hoooo boy, did I get started early on the old vino, and to atone for my unproductive, hungover state I decide I will go to the gym for the first time since the bomb. But first school, then breakfast. Not everyone is sending their kids back yet—in fact, some schools haven't reopened—but we want to act like everything is normal, so to school Loretta goes, holding my hand.

Then Kelly and I are standing in the kitchen. I make coffee. She eats cereal. We continue an ongoing conversation: Can Loretta dress up as a shark for Halloween?

"A blue T-shirt?" I say.

"She needs a good fin," Kelly says.

"Attached to her head?" I say. "Or to her back?"

Then I check my email and remember a note the school had sent before the bomb about a new policy. "Costumes are to be fun and child-friendly so please avoid any scary types of costumes. It will be a fun time for children and adults alike."

No shark. It feels good to follow a rule. So maybe she will dress up as a doctor, like my sister in Illinois, where Kelly's from, where all the grandparents live, where a spare bedroom awaits us if it comes to that. I don't want it to come to that. But I also don't want for a second to imagine running past mangled cars, a girl in my arms. There is this truth that Loretta will grow up and when bad things happen there'll be nothing I can do. Except everything. You know?

Later that morning, Kelly is reporting and I'm at our subterranean gym. I take my usual spot on an elliptical machine, which feels harder to climb, and I look up at all the monitors tuned to various news channels, most of which air tape of the bombing, looping it over and over. Politicians utter their incendiary words, the protestors at the funeral for the intelligence chief throw rocks and sticks, and then the army fights them back with clubs and tear gas. The tape loops again, and the black cloud of the explosion reaches into the sky, and people are dead and the politicians mouth their words and the rioters pulse and then the gas sends them scattering.

I change the station but find more war. On National Geographic there is footage of French villagers fleeing the approach of the German army in World War II. Women and children teeter around on bicycles, diving into a ditch when a tank goes by. Buildings explode and young men in Europe look like they'd rather be at a bar or anywhere else and yet they are wearing uniforms and shooting at each other.

Two women beside me are also watching war. A tank roars down a street, but this isn't France, this isn't archival footage from World War II. This is Syria, a couple hours' drive from where I am right now—climbing and climbing in place—dreading the fact that Kelly will soon enough set off again.

Then the younger woman turns the channel to Fashion TV, skeletal beauties on a catwalk. I envy her ability to think about something else. The old lady on the machine beside her, who might be the woman's mother, continues watching the darkness unfurl, and maybe, like me, she is used to handling delicate things all day, such as a little girl's warm hand, and thus, like me, she has a certain tolerance for routine and the occasional persistent need for a tender touch and this requirement of patience in the face of adversity. On her screen Syrian rebels are firing shells into the air, and then the old lady gets off and sobs. I can't help it, I sob too.

Outside there's a white hibiscus folding in on itself. The taxi guys smoke cigarettes and gossip and listen to the radio. The water is choppy. There's a stiff breeze. I search the sea for the blue-gray foam of a military ship. Can I just be honest and say that, actually, I don't want to leave Beirut? That I am really proud of the work Kelly does and mildly proud of the writing I have begun doing. At least we are in the same country, engaged roughly in the same project. It seems monstrous or at least impolite to complain, to worry about us when so many have it so much worse. I just wish Loretta had a bigger voice, perhaps for no other reason than she would be a tie-breaking vote in our little family of three who live in Beirut, next to Syria, where Kelly and I are doing great except when we are not. We both want to stay, actually, but we both know we need to go.

It's time to pick up the little girl from school and at an appointed time on a corner not far from everything, I meet Kelly so we can get her together, two adults guiding a little girl through a city. It's hot on the Monday afternoon following the bomb and when Loretta emerges from the school, she has what looks like dark circles under her eyes. Like a sack of vegetables that has been gently tipped by a person who was not fully paying attention, she collapses into Kelly's arms, all carrots and celery. How, if at all, did the administrators, teachers, and kids talk about the bomb at school? Wondering this, I notice Kelly huffing and puffing, so I take Loretta's bones into my own arms. We climb the hill together like this, carrying our tired child through city streets, past the police station and the old buildings and the traffic and the heat and the grocery store and the place where she always likes to pick a flower, and Kelly and I talk about how sad it will be to say goodbye to this. But this is real—not some late-night fantasy, a hilarious caper like driving all night from New York to New Orleans or from Phnom Penh to a beach in Sihanoukiville—a fast-moving Middle East situation involving blood and guts and plane tickets and fists full of cash and Kelly's body armor and a three-year-old girl and evacuation and exile. Our hand is being forced. There is no joy or spontaneity, and I am toggling between rage and resolve, sadness and exhaustion. I pause to imagine the family who will replace us. Because replace us some family must. This never ends. The characters just switch places.

In our kitchen, before Loretta's nap, we talk through the mechanics of leaving. Overhearing our un-careful words, the little girl picks up on things in a way I don't totally understand. "If you don't bring me," she says, "I'll have no parents."

She cocks her head.

"Honey, we'll always be with you," I say. "You'll never be alone. I promise."

She eyes me warily.

In the bedroom, I sing, "Goodnight Sweetheart, Goodnight"—with the refrain, "I hate to leave you but I really must say, 'Goodnight"—and with those words I dream up a list of cities. I worry about whether I'll ever break my promise and leave Loretta alone.

Loretta sleeps and I greet our smiling babysitter, who is urging me to leave, to go to the café like I do every day, and so I head out, wanting to spend a few hours in front of a computer, but my neighbor yells after me to stop. This is Steve, who has been here for too many years. He is upset and tired and the father of two kids. The time on the mountain when we built a snowman feels far away. We stand on the street in the sun, staring at each other. He is married to a woman of Lebanese origin, and she is unsure about leaving. Even after the bomb, or the next one, or the next. A whole war full of bombs could come and still, some will stay. ("You never evacuate," an old woman tells us later. She's lived in Beirut for fifty years. "When you evacuate, the bastards win.") Between his wife's local connections and Steve's British passport, they can reasonably assume that no matter what, they'll have options. In 2006, when Israeli jets bombed the city, Steve had the opportunity to board a boat that took British citizens to Cyprus. In 2008, when Hezbollah soldiers streamed into our neighborhood, rattling off machine guns into the sky, they could have driven up to the mountains to stay with his wife's parents. Both times they decided to stay.

"You leaving?" he asks.

"Probably," I say.

He sighs. A motorcycle rips by.

"You?" I ask.

I know the answer.

"Not yet, not yet."

We size each other up. Squint in the sun.

"Well, good luck," I say.

"Same to you," he says.

I walk down the street, head throbbing, thinking about the balance of fear and imagination. I'm desperate to go and can easily imagine the horror of being separated from my family, or worse. But the day is brilliantly sunny, and what if I'm just crazy? I find it both difficult and all too easy to compare myself to my neighbor, Steve. His son is two. His daughter is a few months old. The price is clear but the math is impossible to calculate. So what if the bastards win?

The streets are empty still. One of the few stores pushing goods is a novelty shop: In the window hang witches' hats, pumpkins, and pitchforks, alongside rubber masks of Bin Laden, Bush, Hussein, and Wadi Jumblatt, a local political figure. The man behind the counter has his head in his hands.

At the café, which never closes, having stayed open even during the years of the Civil War, I fire up the laptop and brace for another wave of images and information, of blood and bones. Instead I come across a message from my daughter's school:

News of the explosion reached us a short time before dismissal. First, we made sure that all Early Years children who ride the bus had made it safely to their homes. Then we identified 11 children who ride the 3:30 bus to the area congested by traffic and rescue vehicles. We prepared a temporary place to keep these children in our community lounge, with two counselors. Fortunately, and true to our school tradition, our parents bonded together and took care of most of these children before it became necessary for our staff to be involved.

After school activities were cancelled and the Halloween Dance has been postponed in deference to the tragic loss of life.

If you have any questions or concerns, you may let me know by replying to this message.

I picture a dance and the eleven kids who were stranded in the lounge. I picture the two counselors consoling them. I think about what it means for a school to say we should band together. I think about a Halloween dance, and how I might reasonably reply to this message.

At the café, a woman at a table of what I take to be professors shakes out a mane of long curly hair, lights a cigarette, and unbuttons her tailored suit jacket.

"Your kids even show up today?" she asks, sighing smoke.

"Some," an old man says. He lights his own.

"They leave halfway through?" she says, exhaling.

"I was hoping no—but yes," he says, blowing a cloud. "They were scared."

I sip coffee and stare into space. When I first came to Beirut, I had imagined afternoons like this. I knew Kelly's job obliged her to go to terrible places. I knew there'd be nights alone, days without word. But then her colleagues started dying, killed by gunfire and bombings. I went to a funeral. I cried in a pew. I hoped, made myself believe after years of worry, that it wouldn't happen again. Would you believe that part of me stopped worrying, or that I thought maybe after a certain point I couldn't worry anymore? Do you believe me when I say it's one thing to worry about your wife and another thing to worry about your daughter?

My computer dings. A new message.

"Are you okay?" Kelly writes.

"No," I reply.

On the way home, I stop at Sam's Liquors. A sad-eyed man presides over a small room full of booze.

"They worked so hard to do that bombing, to kill that man," he says, his eyes red from crying.

I set a bottle of wine on the counter and stand there, waiting for him to tell me the price.

"The thing is"—and here he sighs—"you create a team of killers and what do they want to do? They want to keep on killing."

I look back at the shelves. I contemplate what my wife is trained to do. What my daughter is being trained to do. What I am training myself to do.

I place a big bottle of bourbon next to the bottle of wine.

"I'd leave if I could," he says.

He shakes his head.

After dinner, my daughter nestles herself into my lap, putting her hand on my leg. My mind spins: Stay or go, stay or go.

Loretta gives me a pat—slowly at first, then more insistently. *Pat pat pat.* When I put her to bed I lay my head on her chest.

That night, trying to sleep, my heart pounds. We all have a job to do. Kelly loves hers. I've been relearning mine. Our shared responsibility—this little girl—is something we'll renegotiate the rest of our lives. There are no promotions. There are only promises. I know in my heart that staying is wrong.

Then the stillness is broken by a terrific series of concussions. The earth is shaking and my teeth are grinding, and my muscles coil with fear and with resolve. Have they come for us? I roll over, reaching for Kelly, who is snoring softly. In that moment, I believe I will do whatever I must do.

The noise is just a garbage truck. The machine tips a dumpster, letting loose a thundering avalanche of waste.

Then the sound of a plane roaring overhead. I imagine the arc it makes through the sky, the people inside, their luggage packed and tagged, a black ocean swallowing them whole. Then, as I often do when too much is going on in my head, I close my eyes and try to picture a smooth, round almond.

FLOOD-TIDE BELOW ME

Five hundred years ago, when you crossed the East River into Brooklyn, passing through the encampments of what would become Bushwick and Williamsburg, you'd eventually make your way to the ocean, where you'd find clams the size of dinner plates, and where—in the summer of 2012—I spent seven days living with my family in a water-front rental in Broad Channel, Queens, enjoying what seemed like a perfect week and the start of something truly important for all of us.

We lived in the Middle East, where we had a little girl, and where my wife Kelly had become a reluctant war reporter, and where it felt like we might not make it another year. That half-decade abroad we'd always felt anchored by a tiny apartment we owned on the Lower East Side. When we bought it, pigeons had been the only tenants. We lovingly renovated it and then promptly never lived in it again. But knowing it was there gave us an enormous sense of focus. Like, if things got really bad, we could just kick the tenants out and move back to New York.

But with Loretta it was too small for us to ever really live in again, and we'd sold it. And losing the apartment meant we'd lost our focus. Anchor was up. Suddenly, we had a hard time knowing where it was that we belonged, what we should say when people asked us where we were from.

Untethered and reeling and searching for something, maybe we thought that the Broad Channel rental was the first step back, that this tiny house on a canal was a new slice of New York we could call home. In the Middle East, we'd tried and in some ways we'd failed. The house we rented in Queens was a fantasy for the future as much as the Lower East Side had been a fantasy, an anchor for the past and present.

Before the vacation was even up, in my mind, we were already residents of Queens. I got another media job in Midtown, and I took the A train into Port Authority. We surfed on the weekends and fought alongside a new crew of young parents fighting to make the public schools better. We owned a couple kayaks, but we had our eye on a little sailboat. Maybe someday we'd even add a second story to the house?

Then the rains came.

"We are used to thinking of American beginnings as involving thirteen English colonies," writes Russell Shorto, in his masterly history of New York City. "But that isn't true."

The real history of America, he says, was instead forged on "a slender wilderness island at the edge of the known world." In other words: "Manhattan is where America began."

God, to live on that island—or even just to work there—for a while it was to feel like there was nowhere else more important on earth. When Kelly and I arrived in 2004, we were newly married, cocky and malarial, coming off several years of working for newspapers in Southeast Asia. We moved to New York with everything we owned in the back of a Honda hatchback we'd bought for five hundred dollars. I was from a nowhere suburb of Miami and Kelly was from a small town in central Illinois. With the stink of people who'd flown from Singapore to LAX, we jumped in a car and drove for several days straight. We bombed through the Holland tunnel, zipped down curving streets, and met an old buddy of mine standing on the corner of Prince, probably half-stoned and dangling keys to an apartment in Brooklyn where an old futon awaited us.

Not everyone could live in Manhattan. Four hundred years ago, three-quarters of the buildings on the island were given over to the sale or making of alcohol. In the 1700s, the land that now makes up the United Nations was, according to Shorto, a district of African American slaves quarters. The natives encountered by the first New Yorkers were still living a "late woodlands" life and could only gawk at the settlers' magic, things like knives and guns. But soon enough everyone had a knife.

It had always been hard, boozy, and dangerous, and from the beginning the colony was unmatched in the entire world for its assemblage of people from every continent, Shorto writes, while up north they worried about witches and down south they obsessed about slaves. In New York City, regardless of religion or background, everyone was drinking and screwing and making money and eating like crazy. Shellfish carpeted the Hudson and East Rivers, cool creeks ran down what is now the refuse-strewn desolation of the Lower East Side's Cherry Lane. Deer sipped at pools, the sound of leather boots maybe sending one scurrying. The screech of an owl. Life was great. Life was never easy. The best, the worst.

* * *

Our summer in Broad Channel is history. Hurricane Sandy destroyed most of coastal New York City. A few months later, on a freezing day in January, my wife and daughter are in Beirut and I am in New York to visit friends and I plan to walk the fifteen miles from the Lower East Side apartment we've just sold all the way to the house we briefly rented in Broad Channel. I am standing on a familiar block, freezing rain dripping into my eyes, so far from the open ocean of that magical summer. I try to be stoic, but when I see our names as yet unremoved from the grid of buzzers on that apartment building on Eldridge Street, just south of Houston, I am filled with regret. This had once seemed like the center of our universe. We traded the center of our universe for money.

Walking over the Williamsburg Bridge, the same path Kelly and I had taken in the Honda in 2004, I slip on ice and slush and at the bridge's apex, the spires of Manhattan coming into focus through the fog, taking my breath away.

A few blocks away is the South Williamsburg flat we'd called home before ascending to an aerie on the island. Then as now, the neighborhood feels subhuman, an unwelcome convergence of Williamsburg Bridge-exit traffic, a stop on the J-line elevated train, and the Brooklyn-Queens Expressway. A dinner plate left on the counter overnight in our old apartment would be coated in black exhaust the next morning. A cup of soup has spilled its guts under the tracks. It's revolting, like a tiny vulnerable human body has been smashed. Nearby, a UPS guy struggles under the weight of a package and staggers in what is now a driving, icy rain. I've walked about two miles so far. An ambulance rolls through a stop sign, crossing under the tracks, and I swear the old woman inside is moaning.

I keep walking, amazed, really, by how cold it can be, even with two pairs of pants on. I sidle up beside two black guys, one much taller, and they're both walking fast and conspiring and discussing a woman who will buy benefit cards for cash.

"What ya got, six, eight kids?"

The guy stops to think. His buddy waits, their breath visible in the sleet.

"Eight," he says.

They do the math out loud, skipping with delight.

It is crazy cold and I am beginning to get a blister, so I stop at a bar called Goodbye Blue Mondays, where my hands and thighs start to defrost. The barkeep lets me poke around and in the back I am thrilled to find this massive outdoor space, but then I am saddened by the sight of a rocking horse, reminding me that I am far away both from my daughter Loretta and Kelly. I get a beer. The barkeep agrees that, yes, things do change.

In 2006, upon returning home from a fancy magazine's party where I'd lectured a well-known writer and instructed the editor-in-chief to hire my best friend, I dropped my wallet in our lobby. The super found my stuff and gave it to the building's owner, who in turn called me at work. Not knowing better, I admitted to him that we didn't have an official lease. We were soon evicted.

That's when Kelly and I put in a bid on that rat's nest on the Lower East Side. And then all of a sudden we had a mortgage and a contractor named JJ. The co-op board wouldn't allow me or any-one to do any work in the evenings or on weekends, and the place was so small I couldn't really wrap my head around where I'd put all the bags of old sheetrock if I actually wanted to do some new sheetrocking. So all of JJ's work occurred when I couldn't watch, when I was stuck at my fancy job in Midtown. When we decided to take down a completely inessential little wall, the building code required us to involve the Department of Buildings, which obliged us to get an architect and a permit and pay all this money. I came to fear phone calls with 212 area codes. Kelly took to answering our shared cell phone, an angry serpent that always communicated someone's desire for cash or credit.

Then, after five months, it was mostly done—our little Eldridge Street jewel with hardwood floors, a ship's porthole in the bathroom looking out onto the whole apartment, an old farm sink, butcher block counters, and exposed brick walls. Where pigeons once sat above a doorway, we now had a hundred-year-old timber beam. From the bedroom—where, behind some paneling we'd discovered a cleaver that appeared to be smeared in dried blood—there was a decent view of the Empire State Building, if you sat on the fire escape and drank champagne, which we did.

At the same time we bought our place, our contractor JJ bought a place in the Rockaways, and any of my pride in our great deal and smarts and good luck ebbed when I considered that JJ had a two-story house with several bedrooms and a nice yard three blocks from the beach. We had four hundred and sixty-five square feet. True, that part of Queens was an hour away by subway and some sections of it were crime-ridden and the ocean waves were ominously close. But JJ surfed every day and his email address incorporated the phrase "good news." That spring we attended a shrimp boil in his backyard. By that time my job wasn't going so great and the powerlessness I felt about the apartment situation had spread to other areas of my life. I passed out in a bush.

Why had we ever bothered with Manhattan, that horrible island? Years later, sitting there in Goodbye Blue Mondays, my fingers defrosting, I pulled up the photo I'd taken before walking over the bridge. Our names on unit thirty-three—Nathan Deuel and Kelly McEvers. A little slice of Manhattan that had, for a while, been ours.

We hadn't actually lived there in years—we'd been subletting to various Europeans and ne'er-do-wells. But no matter how far we roamed, having that little space meant that New York was still big enough to include us. On a creaky Internet connection, from Saudi Arabia or Northern Iraq or Turkey or Lebanon, I'd carefully read about real-estate trends and sale prices, feeling this sad joy when *The New Yorker* reviewed a restaurant in our zip code.

Then, a few years ago, my dad was having trouble chewing steak that my mom had cooked for her sixtieth birthday. We were in Yemen when we discussed the likely diagnosis, and we were in Doha when he had the surgery, and we were at last getting ready to fly via Dubai back to New York City when his health really started to fail. By the time I got there, he couldn't talk or walk, and he was dead thirteen days later. Struggling to maintain connections, I pretended that New York was home, obsessively following local news online, reading about a new bar my dad and I would have loved. I kept a MetroCard in my wallet and set my weather to 10002.

Then suddenly friends back home were having kids and wanting more space and making more money, and everyone we knew left Manhattan, even our corporate lawyer buddy. If we ever came back, not just for a visit, but really came back, where would we go?

I'm walking again, all the beer gone, and my face is a wall of frozen tears or sweat or snot. The train rumbles overhead and I am entering my fifth mile walking across New York. Childcare this morning at a facility in north Bed-Stuy is a Mexican-looking guy in a black button-down strumming a guitar to a room of ten kids my little girl's age. I watch through the window for a while but I begin to feel like a creep and also I am sad and cold and tired, and I consider how much a room would cost at the Neptune, a grim little hotel just a few blocks down by the tracks. I buzz the buzzer and a thin black man with rheumy eyes and a grey Afro opens the door. He gestures up a set of rickety stairs, where I talk to an old lady in a flower-print dress. She eyes me warily and says she has one room left. How much? It's seventy-five dollars from six PM to eleven AM, and it'll be one hundred dollars if I check in now. I smell like beer. I walk on. At the window of a pharmacy down the block a woman in a fur hat is looking longingly at a display of adult diapers.

In August 2012, we took our sixth—or maybe our seventh—trip back to New York City since we'd moved overseas. It was the peak of the city's annual stink, when a deep whiff on an F-train platform could cause nausea, but it was the only time we could swing a visit. I'd arranged a rental of my friend's place in Greenpoint—a neighborhood in Brooklyn—but Kelly thought we could do better. She really didn't have time to look herself, but she wrote me reminders, even when on assignment. *Let's stay somewhere nice*, she'd write from a hilltop village in Yemen, *that doesn't smell like garbage*.

I began looking at rentals in the Catskills, but I recognized none of the town names, and then I discovered it would take hours by car to get to any of the rentals from New York City and perhaps several days if one was going to walk. I even found one with exposed beams and a screened-in picnic enclosure near a bubbling brook and a stove that looked like you could boil a bear on it. Then I looked the town up on the map. It was a hundred and fifty miles from Manhattan.

I found the whole Fire Island and Hamptons thing dispiriting. I did not feel like a guy who shopped rentals anywhere, let alone on such august spits of real estate. One place with great photos of a lovely house was a "share," in which you got a bed in a room with two bunk beds—along with something like twenty other people. The cost for the week included unlimited food and drink, which seemed amazing. "We got all kinds of chesses for your sandwich," the post read. "We got pepper jack, Munster, cheddar, Swiss, American." As proof, I suppose, there was a photo of a tray of cheeses, beside which was a crushed Coors Light and a bikini top.

I dimly remembered, maybe in 2009, reading a newspaper story about a bunch of publishing people who went in together on a little shack, maybe in the Rockaways? On maybe Beach 90th Street? The writer said there were screens in the windows and creaky thin beds, but he also said it was a few blocks from the beach. One week I logged into a site called Airbnb and searched for "beach," which turned up an ugly studio in Bensonhurst. Another time, on Craigslist, a search for "ocean" gave me a dark two-bedroom in Bay Ridge, "right near a Crab Shack!"

Why did the Rockaways resist me? In the Middle East, the day of our departure approached, and I was certain we'd never find anything. Why did we deserve something so special, anyway? New York was cruel. Maybe I'd dreamt up that story about the publishing people and the Rockaways? Fucking publishing people. Fucking New York.

In May there was a gunfight on our street in Beirut and Lebanon stank and it was hot and a motorcycle backfired and my heart leapt and my eye wouldn't stop twitching and after all Kelly's hard work, after her challenging me to find us a cool place, I had to admit we'd probably end up back in Greenpoint. Which wasn't that bad. Not bad at all.

Then, out of nowhere, there it was. A listing for "Beach Cottage in Broad Channel." I couldn't believe it. The place was right on the water, near a stop on the A train, just a bridge inland from the Rockaways. The house had a deck and a dock with two kayaks and a view of the sunset over Jamaica Bay. It had an outdoor shower and smart-looking chaise longues and tables made from old tin signs. It had a giant grill; a set of outdoor speakers; and tomato, mint, and pepper plants. Inside was an airy space with a big kitchen and breakfast bar, a nice desk, a giant but tasteful aquarium, a long couch, two snug bedrooms, and a bathroom right out of Kelly's dreams—clean and big and bright white.

Before being settled by Europeans, Broad Channel had been Indian land, crisscrossed with footpaths and stacks of spent oysters and clamshells. It would have taken the first Dutchmen more than a day to get here from the southern tip of Manhattan through the brush and the forest and required a boat to cross the river. But it would have been worth it if any of them had taken the time or had any reason to leave the island, and they'd probably have been as excited as I was to get beyond the rivers and the bay, so close to the crashing waves of an immense and improbable ocean.

And the price wasn't that bad. I wrote the woman and told her I couldn't believe it and surely it must be taken and then she wrote to say I could have it, and oh, by the way, in case we liked it, it was for sale.

In unlovely East New York, the road starts heading downhill and I hear my first seagull and see my first ruined boat, and the tang of sea is in the air, my feet are frozen and numb, and I board a train to Howard Beach, where I can walk the final ten miles—saving myself from a vast stretch of even more unlovely Bensonhurst. Warming up on the train, I nearly fall asleep, but then the sound of someone opening a soda is like the crack of a rifle. A scowling white woman guards her purse. Everyone is tired. We pass stops called Liberty and Van Siclen and Shepherd.

I size up my fellow train riders, few of whom look all that thrilled to be in New York. I might be wrong, but I think no matter what, after living in New York, you'll forever remember how great it was and forever wonder when you'll go back.

In August, preparing to stay in Broad Channel, we crossed a bridge from the mainland, reaching the island, and the car was packed to the gills with suitcases and coolers and sacks of oysters. Sun glinted off the waters of Jamaica Bay. Living there, I imagined, we could be both city people and beach people. We could enjoy the benefits of a metropolis while enjoying the privacy and freedom of our own backyard. We could ride our bikes to Brooklyn, but we could also paddle to a thing called Shelter Island.

Kelly had recently crossed again into Syria with the rebels. She'd lost colleagues to government shelling and worse, enduring stretches of eighteen-hour days, seven days a week, for months and months. The Middle East felt far away, and it was such a relief to see the wide swath of coastal forest that makes up the wildlife refuge bordering Broad Channel.

Then we rolled past the first sagging houses, and I tried to ignore the trash and the brief commercial strip consisting of a bar, a gritty nail salon, another bar, and two delis.

What did I expect? This was New York City, after all. No big deal.

Then: How could I have been so stupid?

Along each block, I could now see shallow, muddy canals running between single-family houses in various states of decay. At the far end of the island was the bridge to the Rockaways, where a mix of homes, public housing towers, and sand would attract millions of New Yorkers each summer, only some of whom knew how to swim. We hooked a right on Twelfth Street. An abandoned car sat in a weed-choked lot. A Rottweiler nosed through trash. A few homes seemed to be sliding back into the sea.

Then, there it was: our little yellow house. Our daughter squealed and ran up the front steps onto the porch, making quick work of the gate. I dashed to the front door, realizing we'd made no formal plans with the owner, Nicole, about how to get inside. The door wasn't even locked. Inside were tall, drafty ceilings, walls full of windows, a fridge stocked with milk and butter, and on the deck—a real wooden deck—the very same chaise longues and tin-sign tables I'd seen online. A honk from our car broke my reverie, and I ran back to help with the bags.

Despite everything, I hoped Kelly would like it, and to my delight I found her oohing and ahhing at all the plants and the tasteful picnic table and chairs. I called Nicole to let her know we were happy, and I could hear her smiling through the phone. She reminded me about the kayaks, and she encouraged us to paddle as much as we liked. I walked over to the big red beauties, amazed this was really happening. Just forty-five minutes from Manhattan, we had boats! And a float dock! Which at this point was sitting on the dark mud of a canal at low tide.

That's when I noticed the neighbors, many of whom were staring at me. I peered around the decorative fencing—fairy lights!—and noticed a gaggle of leathery women, hands on sweating cocktails, arrayed around a glass-topped table, openly watching us. It was noon and they were already half-crocked. Dreamily, they took drags of thin cigarettes and said collective, throaty hellos. Then I was addressed by the Captain, a stooped version of Popeye with the same big biceps and watery-looking tattoos.

"You wanna swim?" he said, rubbing his belly. "No problem, I've been doing it all my life."

He coughed into his hand and squinted with cloudy eyes.

"Here, take this—for your kid," he said. I wasn't even sure yet how exactly he knew we had a kid. Had Nicole told him? She had told me everyone was extremely friendly here—and nosy. But there I was, accepting a thoughtful if surprising offer of a vintage red tricycle.

"Thanks," I said uneasily.

Kelly beamed. Then she crinkled up her nose.

"What's that smell?"

I followed her out to the dock, where she leaned over and stared at the inky water flowing into the bay. I was relieved to see the spent shells of ancient oysters and clams. But there was probably a lot more under there I couldn't see.

Kelly volunteered to buy groceries while I put Loretta down for a nap, and later that afternoon she returned with bags full of smoked fish, Russian sour cream, fresh greens, kielbasa, and corn, which we added to all the stuff we'd already brought: wine, dark rum, a bunch of ginger beer, five pounds of oysters, and five pounds of clams.

She looked through the sliding-glass doors.

"It's actually not that gross," she said.

I was willing to settle for "not that gross."

The next five days were a happy blur. Our friends came. How could they not? Even the guy who'd just had surgery to repair his detached retina came. I was high as a kite and asked him if it made him feel old to have a detached retina. He said it did.

Loretta learned to ride a tricycle that week. She'd been terrified of her pink Huffy back in Beirut. Other things became possible, such as smoking weed more often than I had since I was in college, yet I felt completely at ease, except for a vague concern that someone might fall into the water. One morning, an old friend's girlfriend and our clumsiest pal went out together on the kayaks. She paddled uneasily, he cackled deviously. When they didn't return for a while, her partner started pacing—they were late for a wedding. Then the pair paddled up, hooting and hollering. In the rising tide, they'd maneuvered into a shoal of jumping fish.

In a little kiddie pool filled with water, a staggering number of children from various couples sunburned together. It was hard to believe how quickly we ate all the clams and oysters, how many trips we took into the bay in the kayaks, that magical feel of salt and sun on your skin, all of this a few blocks from a train that stopped in Manhattan. Toward the end I broke a precious glass, and in my frustration, I kicked the little pieces down through cracks in the deck and tinkling into the sea. I hadn't even realized the water was literally right below us.

Could we live here? At the time, I thought we could. Kelly and I even came as far as discussing the details of a new mortgage. But I had to admit Nicole was probably asking too much money. And though Popeye had been sweet to lend us the tricycle, we hadn't gotten the friendliest reception from the various teenagers lurking around or the rough-looking guy who revved his Trans Am each morning or the Korean guy who had a ten-foot chain-link fence surrounding his fortress of a house down the block. The lots were packed in tight, no room to breathe. Moreover, the city was planning to lift the streets several feet, a noisy and lengthy process, owing to rising seas and a sinking island.

Five months later I am walking to the same house and passing a FEMA disaster relief center. Two men outside look dazed. Their jeans covered in mud and plaster dust and paint, they hold cups of coffee and both look like they might fall over from exhaustion. A star-shaped painting nailed to a nearby electrical pole says, *Keep on going!* A house in the five-hundred block has an official sticker affixed to the front door that says, *No Apparent Structural Damage.* As I walk further I see that every house has a sticker from the Department of Buildings. The red tags indicate demolition.

Then I get to the little yellow house we rented. *Our little yellow house.* I knock and Nicole greets me wearing snow boots. She invites me inside. She's a wiry blond, maybe five foot seven inches, wearing sporty clothing and an amount of makeup that is more than the none you might expect, given the circumstances, and she begins talking fast. I'd last seen her from a moving car driving up as we pulled away. But that house! It had become like an extension of our bodies, a place Kelly and I had dreamed about and discussed at length. The sight of it in this condition—gutted, foul—takes my breath away. Rather than the light-filled palace that had been the stage of so much delight, there is exposed wiring, an angry spray of black mold above a flood line high as your ribcage, yards of raw plywood, and the palpable hum of heartache. Ocean and rain raged in through the same sliding-glass doors that might still have had my daughter's handprints on them. I think I Windexed them before we left, but I'm not sure. It doesn't matter anymore.

I am covered in sweat from walking all day, and mostly I am ready to curl up and go to sleep, but she is all muscle and nerves and intensity, and she explains how she has—almost entirely by herself—ripped down all the plaster, installed new appliances, shored up the foundation, and reconfigured the house so it now has a much bigger kitchen and living room, but it now has only one bedroom. Where would Loretta sleep?

"Ready to get walking?" she says, rocking on her heels, exhaling, smiling. Then she stoops to inspect the contents of a crate containing her stout white pit bull. She pats the animal's enormous flank.

The dog looks about as excited as I am. Before we go, I look around the room one more time, frantically inventorying everything—wondering what has happened to it, wondering what has happened to me—wanting most of all, perhaps, to climb inside the one source of heat: a wooden pellet stove emitting an intoxicating glow. My feet are semi-functional from having walked all day, a blister festering on my left heel, and the last thing in the world I want to do is get back on the road in the middle of winter to continue my walking tour of the effects of Hurricane Sandy, but Nicole and I had agreed she'd show me the worst of the damage out on the Rockaways. So she rigs up her dog in a marvelously insulated coat, and I have no choice but to follow.

Back in the unforgiving cold, city inspectors in orange vests canvas the street and my daughter is far away and we will probably never live here, and I am walking beside Nicole and her dog, and I worry about its paws because the streets are still covered in nails and insulation and shards of glass. I limp, struggling to keep up.

Nicole recalls how she tried to ride out the storm in her house. The sound of the wind was terrible and things started flying off her deck and large debris smashed into the walls of the house. The lights went out and in a horrible burst the explosion of a transformer lit up the night. She ran with her dog through the rain to a friend's house that had a second floor.

The winds howled and the rain beat against the windows, which began to shatter, and Nicole watched as cars floated by, crashing against each other. She wondered whether she might die. But she didn't, and in the strange morning light, her neighborhood was a ghastly scene of mud and dead fish and broken boards. She returned to what was left of her house, and her knees buckled at the sight. But then she got to work, going for days without stopping or showering, remembering how, among other things, she discovered that her fish tank was empty, because the water had risen above the tank and the fish presumably, hopefully, swam away. Missing, as well, was a thirty-foot boat that had been tied to her dock. And the dock itself.

"Water is a beast," Nicole tells me. "So much can go wrong."

We make it over the final bridge to the Rockaways, which even five months later has the soggy, mildewed feel of an old shoe dredged up from the bottom of a lake. The boardwalk is gone. Rockaway Taco, which I'd read about with envy, is now a soup kitchen. We look at one beachside mansion where an entire half of the house was ripped clean off. A dining room table is still set, as if for dinner, and a hallway closet with no door contains coats still hanging neatly on hangers. A broken water main bubbles. I can smell gas.

It's time to go. I hug Nicole like an old friend and promise that I will stay in touch.

"I hope you move back," she says.

Months earlier, a taxi was waiting and the September sun was shining and my daughter ran around, and we readied to leave our little yellow house in Broad Channel, Queens, headed back to the Middle East. I loaded bags into the trunk and noticed my feet were wet. It had been a full moon and the day's tide was rising so high that oily-looking seawater oozed onto the sidewalk, licking at the wheels. The taxi driver shot me a look of panic.

"Is this New York?" he said. "I never seen nothing like this."

Just before I put the last bag into the car, I noticed these quick shimmers of light. It was a pod of silver fish, swimming down the street, up and over a sidewalk in the city.

THE ONLY WAY OUT

Imagine my displeasure as I pushed a stroller through the security cordon at the Beirut airport at eight in the morning to catch a flight to—of all places—Istanbul. A few days earlier a car bomb had killed three and injured one hundred. It felt like we were fleeing for our lives, but it wasn't really that at all.

Outside, the sun was just poking through clouds. Inside, men with beards sat around watching *Blackhawk Down* on an overhead monitor. I looked up, watching Americans trying to fight off a relentless Somali horde, the death toll mounting by the instant. Head swiveling, I hoped for refuge; the damn thing blared from every screen. Full volume, no escape.

"Daddy, that's scary," said Loretta, who was three at the time. A charred American was being dragged behind a truck on the TV. Kelly was in Doha, hanging out with the Syrian rebel government in exile. On screens all around us, a machine gun ripped a young Somali fighter in half. I grabbed my daughter and walked away. "I don't like scary," Loretta said, looking over her shoulder. "I like nice."

It was my first trip back to Istanbul and I wasn't happy; when I'd lived in Turkey, I hated that city's megalopolis, with all the damn yelling and the construction everywhere and all that new money and boats roaring around and the insufferable whirling dervishes twirling around insanely and the worst morality-taxed wine you could imagine. So when we finally moved to Lebanon, where life was allegedly much better, with better wine and good friends and a small-town vibe, it seemed like we might finally achieve the right balance between risk and reward, quality of life and quantity of action. But the calculus felt muddy after our street became the site of a massive shoot-out and a big bomb detonated in the fall. So, with the opposite of enthusiasm but with the conviction of the crazed, I was moving back to Istanbul.

I guess we shouldn't have been too shocked. It was two years since Kelly had taken the posting in Baghdad, which was a shitty thing for everyone involved. Except Kelly kind of liked it—even with the mortars raining down and the absence of a grocery store she could safely visit without worrying about the unlikely but still daunting possibility of being kidnapped by Al Qaeda in Iraq and the inevitable head-chopping that would follow. She liked it because she was doing something important, working as a reporter, meeting great colleagues, changing the world. I visited her in Baghdad once—Loretta safely back in Istanbul with my mom, who was babysitting while I was with Kelly—scared out of my mind to sit outside by the Tigris one night among Iraqis and eat a fish dinner. My fears seemed justified when a half-hour into the meal a mortar landed nearby, making me yelp with fear. And yet none of the Iraqis even flinched. In the morning, a rocket turned a nearby apartment complex into dust—and despite my fear and my inability to process it all I could still see the hazy shape of the battle-scarred reporter Kelly was becoming.

Turkey shouldn't have been so hard. But somehow, during those months I was alone with our daughter, I was miserable and pissed and feeling sorry for myself, like I either didn't have the time or the ability to enjoy a big fabulous city. I felt tied down by a toddler. Completely emasculated. Floundering. The couple of times I arranged for a babysitter and went out, I thought only of Kelly in Baghdad. What was the point of trying to enjoy myself when the world was such a mess? I felt guilty and went home early.

In Turkey, whenever I went out with Loretta, it seemed there was something incomprehensible about a man taking his little girl out for a walk. Other men would look at me strangely. Women would come up and pat my arm, sadly. Not speaking enough Turkish, I couldn't be sure, but they seemed to be saying, "We're so sorry your wife is dead." In their eyes that may have been the only possible explanation as to why a man was outside during the day with his little girl.

Then we all moved to Beirut with its good wine and we all finally lived together and we had the time and inclination to do things, like go hiking in the mountains or to start writing again, to see life as something more than a strange limbo of waiting and worrying. Alas, even in Beirut, violence was a constant, whispering promise that nothing good could last forever.

Evacuation: I had practiced it enough in my head, imagining what it would look like when we left, when it was time to go. There'd be a rush for the airport, but goons with guns might set tires on fire and the road could become impassable. The airport would be closed and leaving by boat would be the only way out. Western countries might send evacuation ships, as they'd done during the 2006 war with Israel. I'd heard the British troops were fast and nice and professional, but word was that the Americans were sluggish and even a bit dickish. I didn't relish the idea of standing in line with a thousand sweaty frightened people trying to board a boat as gunfire and bombs tore up the city behind us, so I decided to go to Istanbul to make a plan B.

On the plane to Turkey, people looked worried, eyes scanning the other passengers, everyone stuffing their luggage too quickly into the bins, items falling out, babies screaming, the parents sitting down with booming sighs, this ambient impatience for the drink cart to come around, tinkling with liquid calm.

Loretta was excited and antsy. Did she realize what was going on? She buckled and unbuckled her seatbelt, head tilted to hear the satisfying snap of the metal action. Then she yanked the laminated card from the seat pocket and thrust it in my face.

"Say the words," she said, pointing emphatically at an image of a man doubled over, flames licking at the edges of an airplane compartment. The engines outside roared to life.

I absentmindedly patted her hand, looking out over the city for signs of smoke. If things got crazy again, I knew Kelly would be on the first flight back.

"Daddy? Talk to me!" She grabbed my face and pointed it at her. "Talk!"

In singsong, I said as much as I knew. "If we experience turbulence, masks will descend from the ceiling. I'll need to put my mask on first. Then I'll put on yours."

She nodded thoughtfully then picked her nose.

Putting my coat in the overhead bin, I took a good look at the people in front of us: The stocky patriarch, with five-o-clock shadow, a dirty sweater, and the rakish arrogance of a guy who doesn't fly much but never loses his cool; attractive wife tightly packed into a head scarf and a devout trench coat; and their child, small and curly-haired. Through the break in the seats, I could see he had two iPhones and I wanted to be mad at him, to pass judgment because he was apparently so easily amused by such trivial things, ignoring his wife and child—using the panorama function on his camera, or testing his ability to make a friend's face appear pinched with the touch of a button. I watched, unable to look away, as he began to page through a hundred photos from a party in the mountains, maybe a wedding, a big roaring bonfire, all the women in headscarves, and he was completely ignoring his baby and wife, the former of which was whimpering, but he thought it was cool to yuk it up with the guy next to him, who may or not have been his brother. Then I noticed the big scar on his face, his broken teeth, and I wondered if he was a fighter? I recoiled for a moment, hoping he hadn't noticed me.

The plane left Lebanese airspace and the man paged through more party photos with a thick, stained thumb, stopping to admire a woman in a pink headscarf showing off a round, shapely rear end.

Then, with a flick, he opened up some kind of war app. The screen of his phone filled with fire and he tapped the middle of the flames, from which emerged the shape of an assault rifle. He tapped the gun again and it fired off a round. He tapped again—BANG—chuckling idiotically, the gun firing loudly—BANG, BANG, BANG. Then his baby began to cry and he didn't even stop firing as his wife got up to take the creature to the bathroom.

I vowed to do better this time. If Istanbul would be home again, I'd try to learn to enjoy it. I'd live in a more quiet neighborhood, I'd make many friends with parents, I'd take Loretta to the finest parks, and I would not allow myself to feel sorry about anything.

* * *

I installed Loretta at a temporary apartment in Beyoglu. I'd had the wherewithal to arrange for a babysitter. Bathed in the sunshine of a city on the sea, it occurred to me as I walked to a nearby grocery for beer and bread how obnoxious it had been to have ever hated this place: one of the world's best, with an enchanting river and seven of the most stunning mosques in all of Islam.

The next morning, I set out to look at places to live. I found it amazing how orderly the metro was, how some guy patiently and professionally sold newspapers without appearing grizzled or war-ravaged or melancholy to the point of convalescence like in beautiful, broken Beirut.

On the bus, the handsome woman next to me checked Twitter on an iPhone so new it looked like it was made of ice. Parts of the city seemed like architectural models for some Scandinavian super-city of the future. I was impressed by orderly traffic, the clean paint on the medians, oceans of grass, all the gates and fences, the computer that took the fares beeped and blipped.

Then we passed an army of lawn care professionals busy tending a nondescript park that if in Beirut would be considered one of the city's best. Here in Istanbul it was little more than a glorified median. The men wore vests and wielded the orange bodies of brand new machines, expertly clipping hedges, shaping bushes, pruning trees. The bus stopped at a station for the nearby technical university and I was getting ready to make some grand conclusion about how advanced Turkey was before noticing one of the lawn care guys taking a very long piss against the wall.

The real estate agent was the same one I'd used years ago when I first moved here, and she looked older and wealthier with a tighter and polished look. I watched her shake the bangles on her wrist and tap out emails on a BlackBerry. As we puttered around town in a rented van, I tried to decide whether or not she'd had plastic surgery.

I loved the three-bedroom place with the amazing sea view that she showed me in Arnavutkoy. A house in Rumeli Hisari needed work, but each of three floors had views of the Bosphorus. Whether we actually moved or not, I was doing my best to conjure up a life here. It had required leaving my kid with a virtual stranger I hoped would be nice to her. I was tired and annoyed and I hoped the stars would align.

The next day, I took Loretta to visit schools. One had bunnies in a cage and fish in a pond, and in the kitchen a Turkish woman stirred a vat of mashed potatoes big as a bathtub, and the air was clean and there were trees everywhere. Loretta clung to my leg and then warmed up to the situation and began to play with the kids. She ran off as I talked to the administrator, and when we found her she was putting her shoes in a cubby hole in preparation for story time, as if she'd already enrolled. As if we'd already made up our minds. The other school was in a refurbished Sultanate-era hunting lodge, in a forest, next to a castle, which had protected this city for a thousand years. In this wooded glen with the waves of the Bosphorus twinkling in the distance, it was easy to forget that Turkey had its own problems. Istanbul sits on a major earthquake fault line, Kurdish separatists have been all too happy to blow up a bus or two, and a rising disparity between rich and poor means the occasional tourist gets murdered.

The sun was sinking and Loretta very much wanted to take the bus back to Beyoglu. It wheezed to a stop, but I could barely get the stroller up and through the doors. I needed help, but the Turks weren't super eager to extend a hand. Then the driver started pulling away—the stroller and Loretta half inside—and

I screamed and people couldn't ignore me anymore and finally a woman picked up Loretta and held her in her arms.

I sat in the sun, suddenly realizing there was no way we were moving back here. Kelly wouldn't be able to abandon the Syria story, and I wasn't ready again to be apart from her for months at a time. Coming here had been a smart move to the extent that now I knew: if somebody blew up our building in Beirut, we could build a new life, if we absolutely had to, by coming back here, by going backward. But that time hadn't arrived. Not yet.

The bus rocked back and forth, and in the sun-bathed calm of a mid-afternoon ride we both became sleepy. Then a car cut off the bus, and my daughter—who had been half-standing on her seat, mouth open at the majesty of it all—went flying. Just in time, I held out my arm, stopping her fall.

5

CAVITIES

It's Monday, and I am barreling on foot through the thick funk of morning commuter traffic, crossing the spine of Hamra. It's another hot, crazy summer—and as the rockets go back and forth overhead and the snipers grease their guns and everyone waits for what happens next, I have to admit: after five years in the Middle East, I still care about my teeth.

At the clinic, I wipe sweat from my brow; the lady at the front desk is wearing an alarmingly tight mini-skirt and blouse. It is somewhat painful to watch her walk because the basic necessities of human mobility require that bones pivot and tendons stretch and hips swivel. I am waiting for her green uniform to explode, to be blinded by a whiplash of teal fabric.

I take a seat in the throne. Around us are plate glass windows and a stunning view of another way Beirut is being demolished. The thud of shovel-loads of Ottoman-era bricks slam into a dumpster. One day, sooner or later, even the strongest walls come tumbling down. In a town in which nothing was ever higher than the old lighthouse, there are steel towers and no longer parking for anything but luxury cars.

"You'll want to wear these," the dentist says, handing me goggles thick enough for welding. "There's probably a lot to do."

The assistant hovers to my right, sluicing water and whatever else from a mouth I open as widely as possible. In the mountains, they're firing guns in the air to celebrate the dead. There's still talk of chemical weapons. John Kerry, back from vacation, has issued a statement. John McCain has some opinions about kilotons. At a certain point, focusing for an alarming amount of time on a rear right molar, I expect the exasperated dentist to break out a pickax. How complicated could it be? A worrying flood of liquid sloshes around back there, and I begin to lose feeling. I imagine a family of eels has taken root in some hole, that they are striking back—affronted by the pick and whirr of tools and strategy—all but ready to claim harassment or eminent domain, to complain or ask for more, something different.

It's crazy, really, what we're willing to endure. How we submit to such treatment. The pain, the length of it, the arbitrary cruelty (or not) of a stranger who is in theory working with your best interests in mind. Sitting in a chair, you want a good and thorough job to be done. What good, after all, would half an effort be? You want the job done right, whatever that job is.

There are people out there who wait or give up. Because it is a kind of torture—this feeling of half-drowning and the sound of the drill. In theory, you wouldn't wish the experience of being at the dentist on anyone, and yet we do it to ourselves, and worse, we stand by, watching bad jobs done to others. (In dungeons all around us men and women open wide.) In a world where there's self-preservation, the ability to aid others, and the thousand ways we can let each other down, sometimes I wonder, Why not let it all decay?

Outside, the construction continues. I think about the set of teeth I encountered at a museum on the campus of the American University of Beirut. "This had been a very large man," the placard said. In a skull sawed in half, six bottom front teeth were held together by an intricate lace of thin gold wire. He had been a chief. Thousands of years ago, this large man had commanded the kind of power to help invent or at least advance a whole new way of thinking about what we can or should do in order to keep going. Not enough probably for steak, but certainly for some nice bread. Today, we can feed a man through his nose.

Then the woman removes my bib. Into a yawning drain I spit blood. I pay my one hundred dollars. I walk out into a fearsome heat. It's Beirut in the summer of 2013, and a BMW SUV is double-parked beside a backhoe, which is having trouble swiveling its enormous bucket, blocked as it is by the other machine. It's a beautiful car. Below they are digging a deeper hole into old rock, from which another skyscraper will rise, to be filled by people no more important than anyone else who's ever lived.

IN THE COUNTRY

Ten thousand miles from the chaos of Lebanon and Syria, I'm riding a dead man's bike along Illinois's Sangamon River, where some years floodwaters cover everything, sending black fingers searching among dirt and oaks and cottonwood trees. They say you can't really live in the flood plain, that it's unsafe. But here I am, having fled the Middle East, wondering, "What's the point of being safe if you don't feel fully alive?"

Kelly was in the Middle East one last time, covering the growing unrest in Cairo, where the military had regained power, protesters were setting the streets on fire, and angry young men were getting shot by authorities. When I got her on the phone, her voice was shaky but threaded with exhilaration. Another afternoon, hoping for good word from her, I paced a carpeted room, clutching a cordless phone, and then realized how much I miss it too: the violence, the chaos, the urgency of life on the edge.

But after five years, we had decided it's time for something new. After years in some of the world's craziest places—Beirut,

Baghdad, Cairo, Riyadh—we are leaving. It is someone else's turn.

Saying goodbye wasn't easy, but with the deteriorating situation in Syria, staying might have been harder.

My first stop in our new life is with family in Petersburg, Illinois, where I'm caring for Loretta, who is now four.

I awake and look out the window. It's all corn, rolling hills, tall pines, and the soft sights of an American summer—a world away from Beirut, or even Miami, where I grew up.

I might have stayed forever on the East Coast. Only by marriage, really, have I come to know these Middles.

A decade ago, I started coming to Illinois, where Kelly's family lives on a lake. After a few years, my own parents started visiting also, and the six of us spent easy weekends drinking canned beer, eating long swords of pork, and cruising around on a deck boat.

After my dad died, my mom came to Turkey for a few months. I thought she might stay forever. We did our best together, missing our spouses, wallowing in grief. Back in Miami, the empty house echoed. Soon after, she bought a place in Petersburg, near Kelly's parents.

My mother has found happiness in Illinois, and I supposed we could too. In the gloom of one of her storage sheds lay boxes from various lives: Miami, Riyadh, Istanbul. I try to lift one, but it's too heavy. In a corner, I find my dad's sleek old Raleigh bicycle. I hop on, pump the pedals, roar down the driveway and sail down a blacktop road.

The miles fly by, and I think about Beirut. After the privations of Saudi and the cold arrogance of Istanbul, it felt like the perfect middle ground, with enough danger and daring to keep things interesting but with enough history and culture to remind us there was more to life than body counts and bravado.

Heading for higher ground, I fly up and down sun-dappled hills, trying to recall that feeling I got each time a bomb went off, that mix of excitement from the adrenaline and the pounding regret for those who had been killed, followed by the fear of what might come next. Of course, there was a time we felt invincible. But 2012 was the deadliest year on record for journalists, and most of these deaths happened in Syria. The first half of 2013 hadn't looked much better.

On the bike, amazed at how fast I can go, I come upon a doe partially hidden in the forest. She holds my gaze, and her tail stands at attention, rigid and white. She's gone in a flash. In the face of danger, I suppose it's natural to want to flee.

But the alternative, to settle down, isn't always inspiring. I pass a row of singlewide trailers, each with its own half-acre parcel of land. One trailer with cracked windows sits on overgrown grass; the lot also has two horses, sleek and rippled with muscle. A little boy our daughter's age digs in the dirt, working a toy construction machine over and over.

There is a blue bird in the middle of the road. It cocks its head. With the sun pounding down and leaves shimmering in the wind, I'm ready to make some sort of conclusion about the merit of slowing down or the peace of enjoying a quiet moment. But it's hard not to feel like we exited our old lives too abruptly, that there was unfinished business. The bird flies away, interrupting my thoughts, soaring into the air.

Eventually we'll settle somewhere. Our daughter will go to school, Kelly will work in an office. I'll cobble together enough work to get by. Together, we'll try to keep the glass in our windows from cracking.

A big farm truck roars around the corner. I hop back on the bike and pedal hard, hugging the shoulder. I'm going as fast as I can, hoping to outrun what's coming or catch up to what's already gone, pumping my legs, trying to go faster than ever. Every day since we left the Middle East, I've been trying to believe everything will work out—here, and in the crazy places we left behind. Just then, the chain pops off, the pedals lock into place, and I roll to a stop.

In the dirt beside the railroad tracks, I throw down the bike in disgust. Walking the rails, feeling trapped, I calculate how long it would take to fly back to Beirut. After a while, the ordinary penetrates. Among the rocks are knots of brittle metal, rusted railroad spikes, an old beer can, and the bones of a shattered fawn.

Sensing something, I look up to the sky. High above, a vulture circles. In the haze of another afternoon in America, I slap at my neck and arms. The bugs won't leave me alone.

PACK IT LIKE A POP STAR

It was 8:30 PM—time for a cup of coffee before I started writing—when my mom announced that she needed cigarettes. It was a midsummer night—weeks since my daughter and I had left the Middle East for the American Midwest. Kelly was still in Beirut, punching the clock on one final assignment as a foreign correspondent. She was planning a big party at a friend's sprawling top-floor apartment before packing up and flying home to us. Ten thousand miles away, I luxuriated on the back porch of a house beside the water, enjoying the sunset with my mom and mother-in-law. The weeks had flown by since we'd left, me wanting to get away from the violence and the heat, thinking and hoping and praying—I suppose—that we'd never have to go back. In the end, amazingly, Kelly had finally decided she needed to leave, arguing for and accepting a new posting in America. I still wasn't exactly sure why she'd decided it was time, and I had a feeling she didn't know either.

Waiting for her, the grandparents and I had developed a routine. We took turns caring for Loretta, coming together every night for dinner and occasionally consuming entire bottles of gin.

"Need anything?" my mom said, jingling her keys.

"You know," I said. "I'll take some tonic."

Several hours later, well past midnight, my mom lit a cigarette. "Don't you want to be there for the final party?" she said.

Suddenly, I found myself typing the words *Beirut* and *flight* and *tomorrow* into Google.

"See if you can book two," my mom said, looking over my shoulder.

I put a cigarette behind one ear, placed another in my mouth, and adjusted my glasses on my face. Each lens was smeared with lime juice and ash.

"Mom," I slurred. "Start packing."

In Amman the next day, we wandered past the brand-new terminals—ceilings soaring to the sky—where lines of Arabs awaited flights to everywhere. The list was a rogue's gallery of cities I'd alternately loved and loathed—Riyadh, Istanbul, and Beirut—places that were already a part of the past. A day earlier, I'd been feeding my daughter pasta. Outside, the desert stretched for miles. And yet going back to Beirut on the spur of the moment for one last blowout felt somehow like the most normal thing in the world. I was relieved when we found a bar where a skinny Arab slowly rubbed a beer glass over and over.

"Can we have two?" I asked, pointing at the tap. The man pulled the handle and a luscious flow filled two mugs.

"Honey, you look tired," my mom said, gesturing at the barkeep, smiling—wanting, I'm sure, to be polite. But doing or saying the right thing wasn't always easy, no matter how good the intention.

"I'm fasting, ma'am," he said. "It's Ramadan."

Exiting the doors of the Beirut airport, I spotted Hussein, our beloved driver and a man who had outrun Israeli war machines with his massive Mercedes—and then I promptly tipped our luggage cart, sending a bottle of duty-free whiskey smashing to the ground. We watched brown liquid disappear into the cracks of the sidewalk.

Outside, the lights of Beirut twinkled and Hussein hit the gas pedal. In the car, all was as ever. "Everything quiet?" I asked. This was a question I always asked when we came back, because I wanted to know if there had been skirmishes. Were the men with guns out tonight? Did I need to stockpile supplies or plan to keep Loretta out of school?

Now I was without child, driving through a city unencumbered by the things that had made me who I was for so many years. It was just me and my mom, tactless and uninformed, perhaps, but ready to party. I stifled a yawn. It was eleven PM. We needed to get our game faces on.

"This is a great thing, this surprise," Hussein said. "But it is a terrible thing you are doing, leaving. None of us want you to go."

At the party, a Belgian reporter saw me first. "Nathan's here," he said. "Nathan's here!" I put my finger to my lips.

Skulking through the crowd, I moved among what felt like a museum of reporters and human rights workers, the people we'd come to know so well, the group who risked everything over and over to tell the story of Syria: There were bureau chiefs from *The*

New York Times, *Wall Street Journal*, and the *Washington Post*, reporters and photographers from the *Financial Times*, AP and Reuters, researchers for Human Rights Watch and the Carnegie Endowment, and among them some of the most important Syrian activists and refugees—people who might, someday, if they could, put that country back together.

For two years, we'd been drinking and crying and trying to live together—all of us fighting to remain human despite the horrific backdrop next door. Some had died. Some vowed never to leave. Some had already split. It felt ghoulish, this trick I'd pulled, reappearing at that moment. I hoped I hadn't made a mistake.

Kelly screamed like someone had jumped off the balcony. Everyone's heads turned, and I held her for a moment as the party fell completely silent, everyone watching us as we embraced, rocking back and forth.

The rest of the night is a blur of apologies for leaving, hugs for returning, and pledges to never forget what was happening here and what would go on without us. My mom danced to songs in Arabic, and I smoked about sixty-five thousand cigarettes.

We sat at the beach the next day, staring at people's kids. For once we'd slept so late that the people with kids were long gone. Having always been on the parents' schedule, we had never before met these thin childless types. They wore aviator shades and read newspapers in Arabic. "Stuff white people like," someone muttered. Then, out of nowhere, a little girl came running. Not much younger than Loretta, she tripped, and we both braced ourselves for the crying that would come. But she stood up, dusted herself off, and ran deliriously to catch up.

That afternoon I cancelled our gym memberships and Internet, collected the final pieces of mail from our post office box, and settled in for a last afternoon at the coffee shop.

I'd gone to this place daily. I'd written these essays trying to make sense of it all. I nursed hangovers, found out about bombings, and cried over lost friends here. I enjoyed the presence of what felt like some of the most enthusiastic young people in any coffee shop I'd ever patronized. Everyone was always working and talking and smoking and trying to change the world, and sometimes it felt like the Tatooine cantina in *Star Wars*.

When I went to pay my final bill, one of the baristas refused my money. He walked around the counter, gave me a hug, and tried to push me out the door. Standing closer to him than ever before—I was always seated when I saw him—I realized for the first time how short he was. Walking out, I tossed a note worth about thirty-five bucks into the tip jar.

"You'll be back," he said.

Kelly and I embraced in the Middle East one last time. Leaving for the airport, the old worry kicked in. I checked the tickets for my mom and I. Because we didn't land in Amman, where we had a ten-hour layover, until one AM, the airline was obliged to offer us a spot in the airport hotel. I allowed myself to imagine it would go smoothly and that the room would be lovely.

There was a long delay for the hotel. We waited with several dozen families in the Amman airport. The oldest man of each family held an identical plastic tote bag, the logo of which didn't register until I noticed one of the oldest—his hair slicked back and a polo shirt tucked into worn but neatly pressed pants—approach the desk. Reaching inside the man's bag, an official palmed a pack of gum, removed four sticks and gave each to colleagues arrayed behind the counter. The old man's eyes narrowed, and then he removed a wallet, fanning out a stack of bills, as if to say, "Here, take what you will." Raising his eyebrow, the official nodded to the man, peeled off a few notes, thought better of it, took more, and disappeared behind a door with the rest.

The plastic tote bags, I realized then, were all emblazoned with the letters IOM, which stood for International Office for Migration. Knowing the region, I could guess where the families had come from: About half were Syrians fleeing the war. The rest were Iraqi Christians quitting the country after another wave of targeted religious killings. They were here and so were we, all of us equal only to the extent we were waiting for a place to stay.

The airport became more and more deserted. Then even the cleaners went home for the night. I went to the bathroom, where some of the refugees were furtively smoking—and I splashed water on my face and saw my reflection, ridiculous in a Panama hat and salmon-colored shirt.

"I'm very sorry for the delay," an official said, not meeting any of our eyes.

In a pack, we finally moved through the security cordon. My mom and I went first, followed by families who shuffled, carrying exhausted kids and hard-won passports and various sacks and bags. An old lady in a headscarf froze, and I wondered if she'd ever been to an airport. Her son held her hand and she calmed down, closing her eyes as she submitted to a scan. A golden cross swung from her neck.

Outside, another young official told us to wait. With the sun long since down, the desert air was cold and I couldn't stop shivering. Twenty feet away, an Iraqi family was attempting to comfort their young son, pushing together bags to make a bed for the four-year-old boy.

Seeing this, my mom took out a fleece blanket she'd made for my daughter. Before I could think to stop her, she walked over to the family and placed it over the boy, who drew it around him. In America, you could imagine a family appreciating the gesture. With this act of public charity, my mom had unwittingly implied to everyone here that this family—dressed in their finest clothing, hair coifed, and the women immaculately made up—had failed, that they couldn't provide enough warmth for their boy.

A bus arrived, and once we were all seated the father stood up, cleared his throat, and made a big show of handing my mom the blanket, which had been expertly folded. In our room upstairs, I tried to explain. My mom lit a cigarette, trying not to cry. I thought about how confidently Kelly carried herself in Beirut, the very fact of our leaving was its own kind of shame.

At the airport the next morning, disgorged from another bus into the harsh light of day, I found it puzzling—after such an intense night—to see travelers streaming all round us as if nothing were out of the ordinary. Some carried Louis Vuitton, others toted the backpacks of college adventurers, and still more arrived by limousine or luxury SUV, hurrying off to important meetings in European capitols.

A new airport official escorted us to passport control, keeping close count, making sure no one stayed behind. Already swollen with refugees, Jordan didn't have room for more.

On the flight back to America, we sat behind Kato, who was tall and blond and beautiful and who loudly told her seatmates that she was a "pop star." She said she'd just been in Israel doing a video shoot. Beside her sat a family of Arab girls—who, compared to the pop star, looked like specimens of a smaller, rounder species.

Two hunks sat across the aisle. I overhead them say to Kato that they were from Tel Aviv, and that yes, they would love to hear some of the pop star's music. Her headphones were too short, sadly, but, yes, they wouldn't mind at all if she sat in their laps.

The Arab girls' harried mom was torn between wanting her girls to enjoy the flight and her growing alarm at the fact that the pop star was now stroking the face of one of the Israeli hunks

When we were up in the air I stared at the onscreen map. All these countries were so close—Israel, Jordan, Lebanon, Syria, Iraq, Saudi Arabia—and yet they were all different enough that they might as well have been the North and South Poles. In some alternate universe, all the people on this plane and in this region could get along, eat the same foods, and we could all live in the Middle East forever. Instead, this flight was a Petri dish of alliances and hatreds, of mass executions and military maneuvers. I couldn't wait to forget everything I'd learned. But I couldn't cue up the amnesia fast enough.

Hours later, I realized the pop star had quietly returned from her own seat across the aisle to her spot on the laps of the hunks, pulling a blanket over herself and the men. Limbs began to work under the fabric, and I heard a sigh.

"What are they doing, Mom?" one of the little girls asked, pointing at the writhing mass.

"Watch your movie," the mother said.

A flight attendant plucked off the blanket, revealing more than anyone was prepared for. With a lot of throat-clearing, the hunks put on sunglasses, and once more the pop star repackaged herself, returned to her seat, and closed her eyes.

"Is it hard to pack when you are a pop star?" one of the girls asked over breakfast, an hour or two before landing on American soil.

"You need tons of clothes," the star said, twirling a lock of blond hair, speaking with complete seriousness. "You need tons of shoes. Lots of makeup. Tons of pills—you know how it is."

The girls nodded. They knew how it was.

The video systems flashed on. On the map there was an ocean between where we had been and where we were going. All I could see was the glowing red dot of Chicago, our destination. The minutes ticked by like hours.

We'd always be whoever we were. As easy as it was to book a last-minute flight, a short trip never took us far enough. On the eve of our new life in America, I had a feeling that everything I'd struggled with the last five years—worrying, death, guilt—would dog me no matter what country we lived in.

Some people clapped when the plane landed, and I clapped with them. In the baggage terminal, I watched the carousel disgorge bag after bag, and it seemed there was more from this flight than I'd ever seen—suitcases piled on top of each other, duffles overflowed the belt, briefcases and overnight bags lunged at anyone standing too close or not paying attention, including myself.

A brown hard case nearly shattered my knee, and I thought about the fact I wouldn't have to pack for a while. I thought about the fact I might not fly again for a whole year. I thought about our new life in California. I thought about my wife, who was almost ready to join us.

I submitted my papers to customs and border patrol. I tucked my passport deep into my shoulder bag, hoping not to see it again for a long time.

I passed into America, where I took a deep breath. Then I spotted my in-laws, who sat at a bar drinking beer. Loretta was perched on a stool, head in her hands. When she saw me, she slid off, ran my way, and leapt into my arms. We hugged for a long time.

"You're here, Daddy," she said. "Aren't you excited?"

ACKNOWLEDGMENTS

There are no guarantees in life—well, I suppose there are a few. In the wake of death and with a fear of more I wrote many of the essays that make up this book. I'd write a million more if I could bring back my dad or anyone else.

About death: Many of these essays are set against a suffering far greater than any I will likely ever experience. There's something unsettling about spending so much time on my discomfort. I encourage you to judge me harshly, if you wish.

Among those in the Middle East—many of whom are dear friends, some of whom appear in this book—I must thank Anne Barnard, Thanassis Cambanis, Leena Saidi, Hussein Saadeldin, Aryn Baker, Tamim Samee, Richard Chambers, Delphine Blanchet, Ben Gilbert, Nadine Rasheed, Sarah Birke, Phil Blue, Abbie Fielding-Smith, Jeff Neumann, Liz Sly, Babak Dehghanpisheh, Farnaz Fasihi, Maria Al-Habib, Bryan Denton, Rima Marrouch, Lava Selo, and many others.

I'm also extremely grateful to the friends and loved ones back home, who wished us well, visited us in various far-flung locations, and who awaited us when we finally came back. Among them are grandparents extraordinaire Kane Deuel, Claudia McEvers, and Steve McEvers. Without them, nothing good could have happened. A special thanks to pals new and old, such as Matt White, John Mangin, Colin Wambsgans, Mihir Kshirsagar, Tamara Jachimowicz, Thiago Bueno, Nick Bredie, and Nora Jean Lange, all of whom endured long flights and longer nights of drinking when they came our way. Tim Heffernan, Suzy Hansen, Lizzy Goodman, Bobby Arellano, May Jeong, Graeme Smith, John Lingan, David Knight, Josip Novakovich, Terese Svoboda, Tony D'Souza, Graeme Wood, Mark Kirby, Rachel Hulin— a writer's life would be more lonely without people like you.

At best, I'd probably have ended up a rambling dad blogger, if it wasn't for the hard-nosed, kind, and relentless patience of various editors, including Rosecrans Baldwin, Meave Gallagher, Katherine Ortega, Mark Byrne, Carrie Frye, Choire Sicha, Peter Baker, Jonathan Shainin, Sarah Hepola, Jane Friedman, June Thomas, Ed Lake, Michael Schaeffer, Greg Veis, Jayati Vora, Sam Haselby, and Tom Lutz, among others. You guys are the best.

For facilities and space, a special nod to Sevil Delin and everyone at the Istanbul Media Pool, as well as to Café Younes in Hamra, and the amazing community at Deep Springs College.

Gigantic thanks to Rebecca Friedman and Bonnie Nadell (and, hell, sorry it didn't work out Jim Rutman!) and to all the guys at Dzanc. Steven Gillis and Dan Wickett took a chance and Guy Intoci and Steven Seighman materialized in the final stretch to make it more than real. Moreover, newly hired Dzanc marketing and publicity maestro Jeffrey Gleaves has quickly blown everyone's mind.

Every once in a while, you encounter one of those infinite dudes, the kind of guy who walks the earth looking all normal, yet he is in fact one of the kindest and most generous readers and writers a body could ever hope to meet. Not only is Jeff Parker in possession of one of the liveliest literary and moral minds I've ever encountered, he has shown himself again and again to care enough and have vision sufficient to help make things much larger than himself. He doesn't have to do these things, yet he does, and the world is luckier for the fact it doesn't seem he'll ever stop. This book wouldn't exist without him.

It's completely impossible for me to string together words adequate to describe my amazing, strong, beautiful, hilarious, badass, world-class wife Kelly McEvers, but I'll try anyway. She's been my best friend for nearly fifteen years—from Cambodia to Rhode Island, Indonesia to the Lower East Side, Baghdad to L.A.—and all along, I never cease to be amazed. Whether you're a Syrian rebel, a Vietnamese marriage broker, an unemployed RV mechanic in Oregon, a billionaire Iranian refugee, or some guy named me, when Kelly is with you the whole world falls away and you feel like you're the only person on earth.

Daughter Loretta, we love you. Don't grow up too fast.

Nathan Deuel
Deep Springs, California
December 2013

A contributing editor to *The Los Angeles Review of Books*, NATHAN DEUEL's work has appeared in *The New York Times, Financial Times, GQ, The New Republic, Times Literary Supplement, Virginia Quarterly Review, The Paris Review, Salon, Slate, Bookforum, Columbia Journalism Review, Tin House, The Atlantic*, and many others. He holds an M.F.A. from the University of Tampa and a B.A. in Literature from Brown University. He currently lives in Los Angeles with his wife and their daughter.